POLO

The Sport of Kings

↑ plus some other people who made a load of cash on the property market!

How to Look Cool Whilst Learning Polo

BY STEVE THOMPSON

meet the cast members

Rupert Muck-Heap	Sylvester Stallione	Juan Wheel-Barrow
(the student)	*(the polo pony)*	*(the coach)*

Copyright © 2016 Steve Thompson

First published in the UK in 2017 by Quiller, an imprint of Quiller Publishing Ltd

British Library Cataloguing-in-Publication Data
A catalogue record for this book is available from the British Library

ISBN 978 1 84689 243 1

The right of Steve Thompson to be identified as the author of this work has been asserted in accordance with the Copyright, Design and Patent Act 1988.

The information in this book is true and complete to the best of our knowledge. All recommendations are made without any guarantee on the part of the Publisher, who also disclaims any liability incurred in connection with the use of this data or specific details.

All rights reserved. No part of this book may be reproduced or transmitted in any form or by any means, electronic or mechanical including photocopying, recording or by any information storage and retrieval system, without permission from the Publisher in writing.

Printed in China

Quiller
An imprint of Quiller Publishing Ltd
Wykey House, Wykey, Shrewsbury SY4 1JA
Tel: 01939 261616
E-mail: info@quillerbooks.com
Website: www.quillerpublishing.com

Table of Contents

Foreword

Preface

INTRODUCTION — 3
   The Difference Between Kids And Grown-Ups — 6
   Physics! — 12

PART I: ~~RIDING GUIDELINES~~ riding like a pro — 15

The Polo Pony — 17

Learning How to Ride — 29
   Balance — 30
   Exercise 1: The Pyramid — 32
   Stirrups — 33
   Accommodating Motion — 35
   Steering — 40
   Exercise 2: Turning in the Pelvis — 44

Basic Polo Riding — 47
   Walk — 48
   Trot — 49
   Exercise 3: Power Trotting — 54
   Canter — 58
   Exercise 4: Trot to Canter Transitions — 62
   Transitions — 62

Advanced Polo Riding — 65
   The Half Seat — 66
   Exercise 5: The Half Seat — 68
   Exercise 6: Accelerate / Decelerate — 70
   Efficient Turning — 74
   Exercise 7: Circles within Circles — 75
   Changing Direction — 76
   Exercise 8: Changing Direction — 78
   Versatility — 80
   Exercise 9: Sink left / Sink Right — 82
   The Tube — 84
   Exercise 10: Chin on Chest — 88

PART II: ~~HITTING SUCCESSFULLY~~ *winning at swinging*   91

Mallet Essentials   93

   The Grip   94
   Exercise 11: Balancing the Mallet   *96*
   The Pendulum   98
   The Plane   106
   The Shots   113
   Intention   120

The Smiley Technique & Grid   127

   Exercise 12: The Smiley Technique   *128*
   The Smiley Grid   130
   Exercise 13: The Smiley Grid   *132*
   The Nearside in Isolation   134

The Hitting Process   139

   The Checklist   139
   Perception and Height Deficits   141
   Making Contact   142
   Exercise 14: Working Backwards   *142*
   Hitting Discipline   144
   Accuracy On Distance   145
   Exercise 15: The Clock   *146*
   Power Hitting, Penalties and Pre-Swings   149
   Exercise 16: The Pre-Swing   *154*
   Pitch-Side Training   161

PART III: ~~APPLICATION~~ *scoring on and off the field*   167

Stick and Balling and Hitting Diagnostics   169

   Exercise 17: Stick and Ball   *171*

Playing   177

   Riding Off   184
   Hooking   185

Problem Solving   187

Stretching   203

And Finally…   211

Acknowledgements   216

Preface

Once upon a time I used to have a proper job! I was where you are likely now, earning a reputable living and paying through the nose for a new-found polo addiction! That was over 25 years ago but I still vividly remember living in the 'real world'. The relevance of this (as a previous 'client' and now a polo coach for the best part of my adult life) is that I totally get it. Lessons can be boring and quite expensive, our egos are massaged to the point where we actually start to think we are good players and our belief is that we can have so much more fun playing polo than training for it. Well, wakey, wakey! The harsh truth is that without training for polo we are not playing it at all, merely spectating it from a speeding furry sofa! I will never be able to stress enough that prevention is better than cure, and as a client once introduced me to *The Law of Bad Habits in Polo*: "ten minutes to learn, ten months of frustration and about ten thousand dollars in back to basic lessons to correct", I suggest you stay on the right side of the 'law'!

In my experience, training manuals are notoriously dull, so in an effort to stimulate the senses whilst learning, we've made this book as light-hearted as possible. However, don't be fooled by its humorous theme - this is a very serious and sophisticated training manual detailing the essential requirements any aspiring player **will** need to develop **before** they attempt to play the game of polo.

This book, followed correctly, will save you a lot of pain, frustration and a significant amount of cash by teaching you to function correctly from the very start. Becoming a player is like building a house: only when there is a true and solid foundation can you begin to layer the storeys on top. It's worth considering that a ten goal player has a head, two arms, two legs and a torso - and so do you, so why is it that he can do what he does and you perhaps can't... yet? There are many answers to this, all of which are contained within the following pages. It is a culmination of over 25 years of tried and tested teaching methods which have proved hugely successful to the students I have been privileged to teach over the years. So, I hope you enjoy the ride... and I'll catch you at the other end!

Steve Thompson
Polo Coach, Managing Director of Dubai Polo Academy

~~Introduction~~ before we start

THIS SPORT AIN'T CHEAP!

It doesn't really matter where you go to play in the world, you cannot escape the fact that you have chosen one of **the most** expensive pastimes on the planet.

Congratulations!

And with that in mind there is something else you really ought to consider: there is nothing available at the pharmacy that will ease the depression of a bad day on a horse with a polo mallet.

There. I hope I have set the scene!

The reason for such an outlandish beginning is that, as a coach, I seem to spend an enormous amount of time convincing people to actually learn the easy way, ultimately getting the required results safely and swiftly. The alternative is to try to work it out for yourselves in isolation whilst riding a horse, hitting at a ball and attempting to be part of a team, often all under the added pressure of an audience. It's a big ask.

It really doesn't matter if you miss the ball. It's polo — you just need to *look* fantastic!

So, if you are thinking of taking up the sport, I greatly encourage you at this stage to at least try to get it right from the start by building a true and solid foundation. This will help remove the ceiling from any aspiring player's ability, and to indulge you in a little trade secret here — all the pressure of playing is already off because it really doesn't matter if you miss the ball. It's polo, you just need to *look* fantastic!

Learn the easy way. The alternative is to try to work it out by yourself whilst riding a horse and hitting a ball, often under the added pressure of an audience.

Blatant as that previous statement may be, I live by it. If you are looking good on the approach to the ball and looking good with the swing, then the likelihood is that you will hit it properly and accurately.

TEAM CHAT

Throughout this book, there are constant reminders to focus on **style, elegance, grace,** and **harmony**. The alternative is to adopt a technique without structure, and join the all-too-familiar throng of amateurs thundering around the pitch looking like they've just escaped from an institution!

THE DIFFERENCE BETWEEN KIDS AND GROWN-UPS

For many years, I have been asked why it is that the Argentinians are so good at polo. My response has always been because they start young — very, very young. But that's not the whole answer. More obviously, a child does not have a controlling adult strength and without it, good hitting skills and good habits get naturally adopted really early on.

Kids BEND towards the ball and pull away from the force, sending the energy created down the mallet shaft. Beginner adults LEAN towards the ball, unbalancing the body and ultimately absorbing the energy by gripping harder to the saddle.

The technique a child uses with a polo mallet is not unlike swinging a sling shot from the shoulder: there is no interference with course or direction, and — once the energy has been created — there is a clear channel for it to be released. For a young polo-

playing child, swinging a polo mallet becomes second nature and it is this ingrained familiarity and technique that adult players **must** aspire to develop and commit to muscle memory from the offset.

Ingraining good habits early is the key to success.

Another question is why it is that 80 percent of the polo playing population is rated at zero goals and below. Well, the answer to that one is that right at the very core of their hitting foundation, there is instability. Instinctively, not many of you would go to the top of a ten-storey building if you knew there was a crack in the foundations. Equally you are never going to reach for the high long shots if your riding position is insecure or unbalanced.

Learning to play polo successfully is all about creating a riding technique specific to the sport, and it is the key to allow you to form a solid platform from which you can build a hitting structure. As the old saying goes, prevention is better than cure, and it is a long and painful process to dismantle deep-seated bad habits from a player who has achieved moderate success with a bad technique. Ingraining **good habits and being disciplined and consistent** in the early stages will put you firmly on the road to success.

As the old saying goes, prevention is better than cure, and it is a long and painful process to dismantle deep-seated bad habits from a player who has achieved moderate success with a bad technique.

Throughout this book, we are going to look at exactly what the 'good habits' are and the tricks to learn them. We will also look at a number of exercises which, done in isolation, will allow an aspiring player to 'feel how it feels' to be correct at various stages of each shot or movement.

> Building a true and solid foundation will help remove the ceiling from any aspiring player's ability.

BECOMING A PLAYER

At its most basic, to become a good player you need to fully understand:

> **THE JOB OF THE HORSE in his role as a polo pony**
> *In basic principle, during the game it is the horse's number one priority to keep you both upright and safe, listen to and obey commands taking you to the ball or the play with maximum efficiency.*

AND

> **THE JOB OF THE POLO PLAYER in his role as a rider**
> *The rider's job therefore as a priority is to stay balanced, to deliver concise, consistent instructions whilst allowing the horse the time required to execute such movements and conserve energy where possible.*

Once this partnership is compatible and each party clear about their responsibilities, the rider can then focus on hitting the ball and making the plays. This book aims to take you down both sides of the boards, understanding and learning the foundational skills that will help you evolve over time into useful and safe team players

PHYSICS!

I hesitate before using this word as it could be a major turn off when you have eagerly begun reading a book about a sport immersed in exclusivity, luxury, and glamour, all fuelled with high-octane adrenalin. Physics was also the subject I totally flunked at school, but the reality is that all polo skill requirements fall under this one unavoidable heading!

Gravity, momentum, balance, club head speed, various forces, and pendulums are all grouped together under the 'P' word which I will try not to use again! The trick to hitting a ball in the direction you have chosen and the distance you want is all about creating, storing, and expelling energy at the right time.

However, none of the above is remotely possible to achieve unless you have a platform. So, way before you even start to think about the hitting process, there is a fundamental stage ahead: you need to master the riding element. And as another old saying goes, 'if you can't get to the ball, you can't hit it!' So with this fairly obvious statement at heart, we are going to begin by focussing in total isolation on the riding itself and the unique and specific skills required for playing polo.

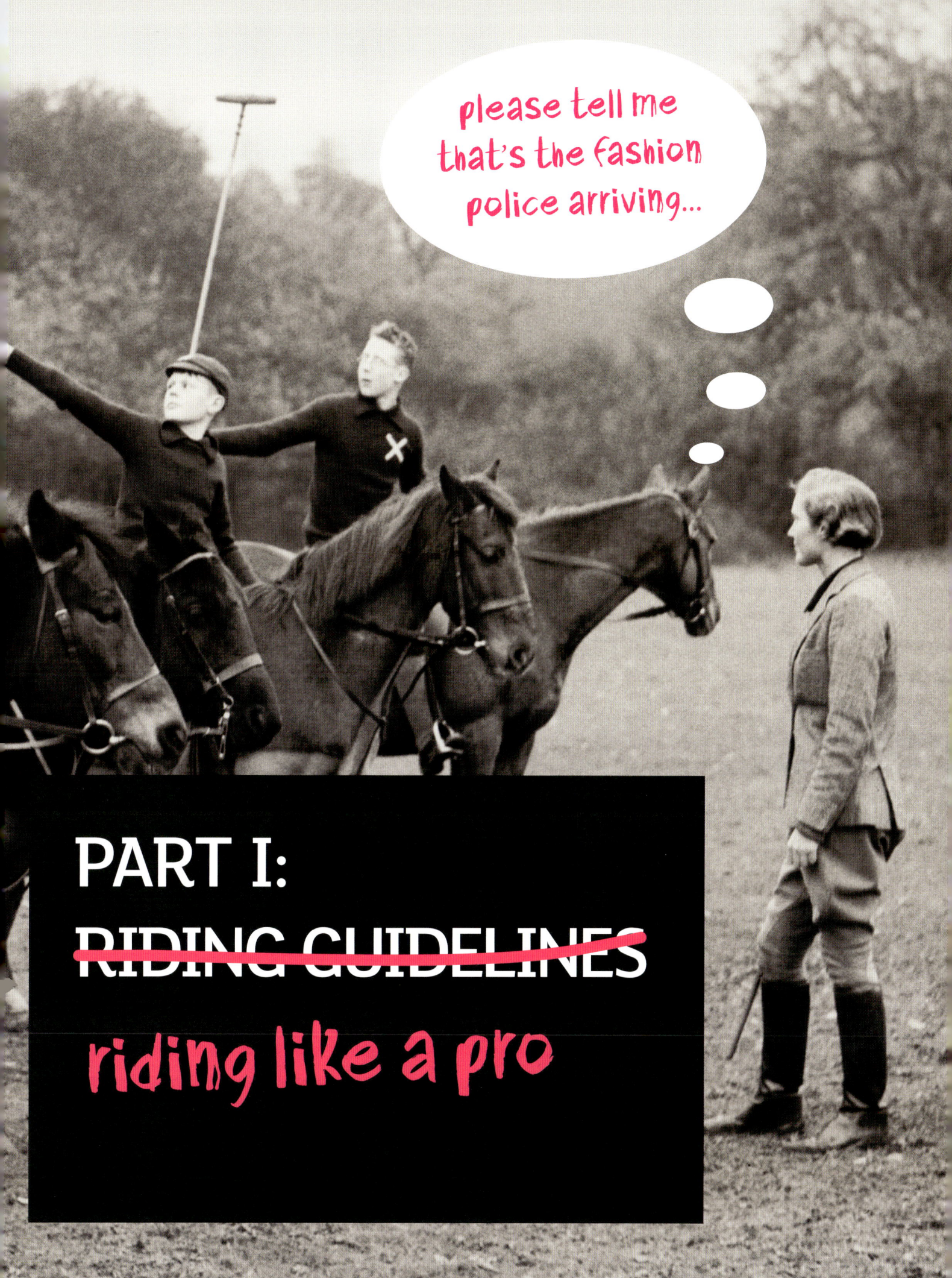

The ~~Polo Pony~~ superhero

DEFINITION: YOUR BIG FURRY MATE WHO CAN TAKE YOU FROM ZERO TO HERO AND KEEP YOU SAFE AT THE SAME TIME – IF YOU LET HIM!

By their very nature, horses are flight animals and they run away from pain or fear. They don't like noise or chaos and are fearful of unfamiliar things. Additionally, and perhaps more importantly, unlike us they don't have the ability to rationalise. Understanding and accepting this should just make us marvel all the more at their absolute courage and trust in their rider in any equestrian sport, but especially polo.

The player/horse combination should be a harmonious one with clearly defined instructions and empathy from player to horse. The fact that any horse allows you on its back in the first place would suggest he

is already submissive and therefore subservient, so he just needs clear direction. If he wasn't keen to please, and he didn't want you on top (as I'm sure some have already experienced), you wouldn't be in situ for very long, that's for sure!

Considering that once you are mounted, a horse cannot actually see you, the fact that he completes his job at all and with such apparent ease becomes all the more astonishing. A horse has monocular and binocular vision so he is blind to you for the best part of the riding scenario. Quite a statement when you consider what you are expecting him to do, all with chaotic, inconsistent instructions from us as players.

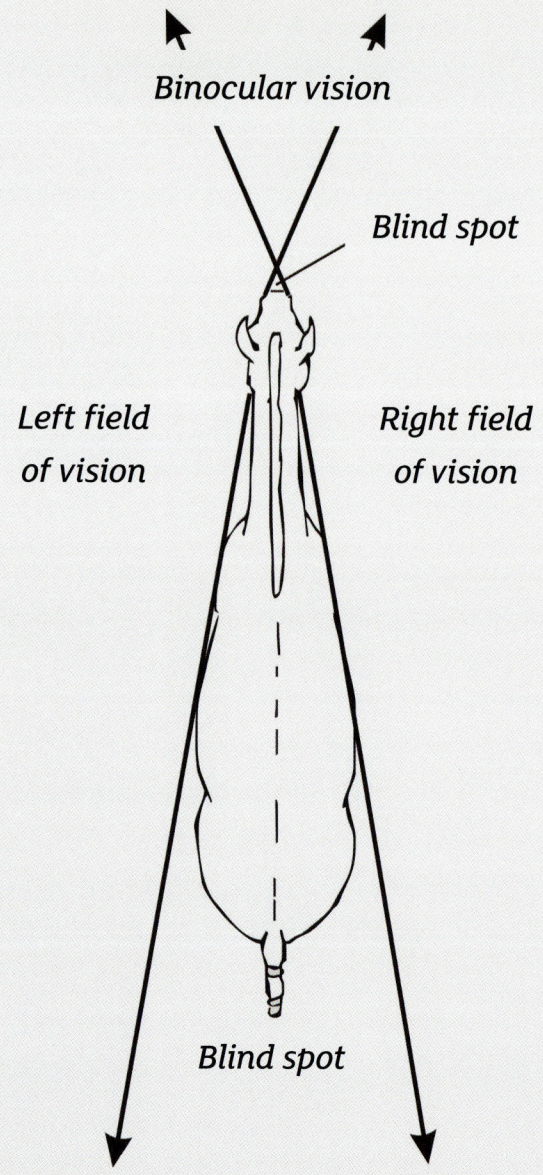

The next thing to really consider is how he does anything at all — and by that, I mean technically and mechanically. All horses are individuals, so we can only answer that one when we strip him of all the man-made aids of saddles, reins, bits and bridles and observe how he actually functions free from any human interference.

The way any horse gallops freely around a field and stops abruptly at a fence before turning and accelerating off is specific to that individual animal. As trainers and players, it is our job to identify a horse's unique movement, to harness his naturally efficient way of doing things and then ask him to do it on command. Only then can we look at improving his efficiency and work towards improving performance.

*The photos below demonstrate the **horse stopping naturally without interference from the rider**. Note how low the shoulders have dropped - quiet contrary to the traditional 'make it sit down' attitude and thought process. It is our job to identify a horse's unique individual movement, to harness his naturally efficient way of doing things and then ask him to do it on command.*

TEAM CHAT

Consider for a moment that a friend has jumped onto your shoulders and is making you run around whilst leaning off, swinging a mallet, kicking you in the ribs and pulling you in the mouth when he wants you to change direction, slow down or stop. Difficult, I think, to stay focussed on the job whilst trying to keep you both upright and balanced. **Now consider the whole scenario again, but doing it with blinkers on.**

Only when you accept the extraordinary display of patience, tolerance, and trust that a polo pony (or any horse for that matter) shows will you ever truly aspire to ride with deserved respect and a real desire to constantly improve your horsemanship.

The great players seem to manoeuvre effortlessly around the pitch due to a lack of interference and minimal but accurate communication to the horse.

The great high goal players seem to manoeuvre effortlessly around the pitch without the drama often seen in low goal polo, and the majority of this skill is down to lack of interference and minimal but accurate information communicated from the rider. Energy conservation is top of the list for good players and the ability to ride efficiently means barely any unnecessary stopping, turning, or galloping; instructions to the horse are almost invisible to the naked eye if the player is indeed a true horseman.

Polo is the strange equine discipline that allows you to effectively 'hire a car for a couple of laps around the circuit' but using that analogy, no one would expect every car to be the same. To take it further, some cars have manual, automatic, or tiptronic gear boxes. Some are heavier on steering and brakes, but generally all will have a steering wheel, a gear box, brakes, and wheels. So the same analogy applies to the horse: whilst the golden rules are all underlying, the trick to riding or playing an unfamiliar polo pony is never assume anything.

*Polo differs from other equestrian disciplines in that it is much more of a consideration of **balance** and **versatility** in the saddle, as opposed to conventional riding whereby the horse is driven forward by the rider's seat and back.*

A polo pony will never subject itself to more pain or discomfort than necessary if it understands what it is being asked to do. So quite simply, **ask**: only then are you in a fair position to apply additional artificial aids.

Now unlike many other equestrian disciplines in which the rider operates the horse by driving it forward with their seat and back, riding for polo is much more of a consideration of balance and versatility in the saddle. Having said that, and not wanting to point out the obvious, a polo pony is still a horse, therefore the basic fundamentals of equine movement really do apply.

When we strip away the image of flying sticks and racing around at speed, if watched in slow motion, the intricate polo pony manoeuvres and requirements on the pitch are actually all unadulterated dressage movements. The advanced manoeuvres of counter canter, flying change, and half pass are all clearly visible. They are just executed in many cases very quickly.

The advanced manoeuvres of counter canter, flying change, and half pass are all clearly visible. They are just executed in many cases very quickly.

DRESSAGE MESSAGE

> **dressage, n**
> *Pronunciation: / dre-'säzh /*
>
> The art of riding and training a horse in a manner that develops obedience, flexibility, and balance:
>
> **ORIGIN**
> *1930s: from French, literally 'training', from dresser 'to train'.*
>
> OXFORD ENGLISH DICTIONARY

1

2

5

6

It has been said that people take up equestrian disciplines such as dressage because they like horses, whereas people aspire to play polo for its sporting nature. However, as both activities require a horse, it is interesting to note that dressage, as the purest form of all equestrian disciplines, is the one that truly demonstrates a harmonised partnership between horse and rider.

To reinforce this *dressage message,* here you can see one of my Academy ponies executing and mirroring an advanced canter pirouette in sync with a top international horse and rider combination. The polo pony I am riding has never been trained how to perform this, but is able to mirror it simply because all horses basically function in the same way.

Whilst speed is often required in polo, **rhythm, tempo, control,** and **balance** are at its very core. Note how precise, accurate, and synchronised her footfalls are during every stride in the sequence.

3

4

7

Amateur polo players often mock dressage as an equestrian discipline…

Pro polo players treat it with infinite respect.

When God created the horse, he built it to ensure maximum efficiency.

Learning How to ~~Ride~~ defy gravity!

'Horse people' spend a lifetime learning about horses, wanting to understand and learn intricate techniques, and looking for that true moment of perfect harmony with the horse. It takes years and years of practice to become a true horseman, and for this reason you need to be realistic about what you will achieve after reading this chapter. No one, after completing this, or any book, will be able to run out equipped with their newfound knowledge, jump on a horse and ride effortlessly off into the sunset! What this chapter will do however, is present you with a greater understanding of a horse's requirements whilst carrying a rider, and how they adapt. It will also present some of the key polo riding techniques and how and when to apply them.

Often it is the case that understanding how something works in the first place is half the battle. So in this chapter we are going to identify some basic principles:

01 Balance
02 Stirrups
03 Accommodating motion
04 Stopping
05 Steering

first five foundations!

01/05 BALANCE

Let's revisit the fact that the horse can't see you. He already has a job to do which is to keep himself upright, and you are about to give him a second one — to carry you. So it will make sense that **balance** is essential and an absolute priority in laying the foundation of a rider's structure. Balance is not something that can be taken for granted in the polo playing environment and there are specific techniques that will allow you to achieve it.

Understandably, aspiring adult players often marvel with a hint of envy when watching small children play polo on adult-size horses and with such apparent ease. However, when you consider the dimensions and proportions of a child riding an adult-size polo pony, it would be

> **Balance is essential and an absolute priority in laying the foundation of a rider's structure. It is not something that can be taken for granted in the polo playing environment.**

the equivalent of an adult sitting astride an elephant! If this was the case, suddenly your legs would be spread much further apart, you would then be wider at the base and much more balanced at the top. Therefore, in fairness to us 'oldies', we have a slightly more difficult job just because we are taller!

TEAM CHAT

To reinforce this message of the importance of balance, here's an analogy that will hopefully make it clearer. Imagine walking onto an ice rink: concentrate on the fact that as you step on to the ice, suddenly everything you do becomes very focussed and 'quieter'. You are very aware of your environment and there are no unnecessary movements anywhere. You would not unnecessarily make violent or jerky movements but more consistent, balanced ones, carefully placing one leg in front of the other, choosing how you place your feet. Imagine now running on the ice and it intensifies the feeling of stillness even more to ensure you are balanced at all times or the inevitable will happen. It is this feeling of no unnecessary movement that needs to be carried forwards for you and your horse to become the ultimate harmonised, efficient machine.

Exercise 1
THE PYRAMID

The best exercise you can do to achieve perfect balance! Start by following these steps:

- Take the feet out of the stirrups.
- Find the deepest part of the saddle and sit in it at the very top of the legs.
- Collapse the pelvis forward and open up wide at the chest and shoulders.
- Now raise up the rib cage as high as you can.
- This will produce a cavity in the midriff which will allow you to lift, tilt and also rotate the pelvis without the weight of the upper body on it – you should now feel quite square and structured.

This new balanced posture will also start to form an essential part of your overall hitting structure.

Consistency is the name of the game at this stage. Instinctively squaring off the shoulders as soon as you get on means that you will always be working with the same riding and hitting machine. A slumping of the shoulders or a weak technique produces inconsistency that will ultimately lead to you having 1,000 variations on how to hit the ball.

The importance of pelvic rotation will become more apparent as you delve further into the book. As the upper body is stretched upwards, equally the legs are stretched downwards. Most people's conformation when astride a horse will now resemble one-third / two-thirds: that is to say, measured from the top of the pelvis, the legs are now longer than the torso, and as a consequence you are forming a pyramid: the most stable structure on the planet.

Remember! **Don't slump the shoulders and stay focussed on your technique.**

The reality is that as adults, playing on an average 15.2hh polo pony is the equivalent of straddling a plank of wood only two feet across. Consequently, this long streamlined position requires slightly more refinement to stay balanced. Coupled with this, you are about to receive energy and elevation from the horse's movement, so unless you have techniques to remain balanced and **channels** instead of **junctions** to expel the concussion of the horse's motion, you are going to bounce!

One-third, two-thirds. By raising the upper body and stretching the legs down with feet parallel to the horse you will create a pyramid, the most stable structure on the planet.

02/05 STIRRUPS are bad!

It is interesting to note that due to the gymnastic demands and essential requirements to move around in the saddle during a game, stirrups are very often lost, so it is essential that you have the ability to continue with your job safe in the knowledge that can ride without them. It is only when stirrups are removed from the equation that you really have a genuine feeling of balance and harmony. Stirrups in the early stages of learning to ride - contrary to popular belief — are not actually your 'friend'. Rather, they mask imbalance and present a platform that leaves the rider with a restricted technique which is absolutely stirrup dependent. Remember, polo is a team sport: your team members are reliant on you to make plays. Having to stop during a game or worse still, actually fall off because you lost a stirrup, is plainly unacceptable!

You can see in both of these images that the player has lost his stirrups but it has absolutely no effect on his intended play.

ALL hitting and riding requirements should be frequently practiced without stirrups purely to highlight the degree of reliance you may have and to identify areas of weakness. Removal of stirrups produces a positive effect on a rider's balance. It's worth considering (especially those who are keen to ride 'shorter' than normal), that when the legs are stretched down you create a one-third (torso) / two-thirds (legs) ratio which in fact makes it almost impossible to fall off.

remember this?

The other positive reason to train without stirrups is that it absolutely encourages lower leg independence. They already have two jobs: accelerating and decelerating. They won't be able to do either if you are using them to stand on! This is essential when asking for acceleration or a stop without compromising the upper body actions.

really important!

03/05 ACCOMMODATING MOTION

We've already established that it's absolutely necessary to remember that the horse cannot see you but only feel you. From this point onwards you will be instructing him ideally with various weight distributions in the saddle whilst gently suggesting instructions with clear but minimal aids from the legs and hands.

In basic principle, anything forward of your body's natural vertical posture line translates to the horse: go, or go faster, and anything behind this line means slow down, stop, or reverse. **Applying this one very concise and clear fundamental means that you have the keystone of all instruction in place and not once have you applied any force or unnecessary pressure to the horse's mouth.**

In front of the vertical: go / go quicker

Behind the vertical: slow down / stop

Anything forward of your body's natural vertical posture line translates to the horse: go, or go faster, and anything behind this line means slow down, stop or reverse. When this skill is refined it becomes almost invisible to the naked eye as the horse learns to respond to initial movement created in the pelvis.

As a result of the upper body tilting forwards, the lower legs and feet naturally swing back, pivoting at the knees. This action will allow you now to be in a position to touch the horse in the general area of the corner of the bottom of the saddle blanket – a really important point to note that **this** is where the accelerator is and not down on the girth as with other equestrian disciplines.

As the horse takes his first step, you have a forward state of motion which needs to be encouraged by pushing the left rein hand forward to ensure there is full and total freedom of head and neck, and the horse knows exactly what it is you want him to do. When a horse receives such clear, precise, black and white instructions, rarely will he disobey – remember he let you on him in the first place, therefore he is already subservient and just wants to do what you ask of him – **so ask!**

Asking for forward motion.

04/05 STOPPING

Having successfully encouraged and moved the horse forward, then you can try stopping. And the golden rule in all instruction is to apply the 'one-second rule'. Consider for a moment the size of a horse and the fact that he must firstly receive information, deliver it to the relevant parts of the body and then balance the rider whilst changing

> **The golden rule in all instruction is to apply the 'one-second rule': it does take a moment for the horse to receive information, compute it and then send it to the relevant parts of his body.**

his leg sequence. Quite a task in itself, and yet as riders it is fair to say that we are all a little too keen to pull up hard and expect an instant result. Only when considering the delayed pain reaction you get when accidently stubbing a toe can you ever appreciate the single fact that it does take a moment for the horse to receive information, compute it, and then send it to the relevant parts of his body.

Lift reins and pelvis and tilt the upper body backwards.

So, you have forward motion and now you can test the brakes. Following that golden one-second rule, all that is required is a lift of the reins to engage the brain, apply a tilt back of the upper body away from the vertical line (centre of gravity) and also lift off the pelvis which is now totally possible because the rib cage is lifted. An added squeeze of the thighs and a push downwards in the heels are all things the horse will feel, and at no time did you interfere with his natural balance.

Most horses will surprisingly stop at walk with these small commands, and almost all will do so after several attempts. The good news is that you now know that the horse actually does understand what you mean by these minimal applications or shifting of weight.

A horse is never going to intentionally subject itself to any more pressure or discomfort than necessary; he generally is happy to oblige if he understands what you want and you give him the time to react.

Half of the bad riding examples you will often see are because the horse had no time to get things right in the first place and was unnecessarily punished by over correction. In ALL cases, you **must** always engage the horse's brain to let him know an instruction is coming by 1) lifting the reins from their handheld neutral position and then 2) simply **asking** and giving benefit of doubt.

Remember, a horse is never going to intentionally subject itself to any more pressure or discomfort than necessary; he generally is happy to oblige if he understands what you want and you give him the time to react.

The question to ask now is why should there be any less obedience if you took these principles up a level to trot, canter and ultimately gallop? The simple answer is that there shouldn't be. The only addition to the equation is the amount of momentum needed to be accommodated at speed – similar to calculating average stopping distance in a car.

You'll see this image repeated several times in the book. It's a classic example of a turning manoeuvre without rider interference.

05/05 STEERING — *don't hold the steering wheel... sit on it!*

A horse's head and neck are there to aid balance. With this in mind, you have to question the negative effect you have as soon as you ask for a quick turn by violently pulling the reins. The only way to allow for complete efficiency is to leave the balance aids alone as much as conceivably possible and use an alternative. And in this instance, it's the pelvis.

> **Visually our two worlds are completely different. The rider's world has purpose and intention: we see neck, ears, reins. The horse's world is what he can see in front and at the side and is listening and waiting for instruction. We *see* everything; he *feels* everything.**

It is fair to say that visually our two worlds are completely different. The rider's world has purpose and intention: we see neck, ears, reins. The horse's world is what he can see in front and at the side and is listening and waiting for instruction. We *see* everything; he *feels* everything.

Now of course this idealistic view of riding is all very well in the perfect world, but of course *horses for courses*, excuse the pun, and every scenario is different.

To ensure I don't miscommunicate this message, there are of course plenty of times when pressure IS applied to the reins which will have a direct effect on the horse's mouth, leading to a change in its head carriage and ultimately its balance. However, with experience you will instinctively know how and when to apply it depending on whether a horse is pulling out of disobedience or other negative factors such as discomfort or excitement, or whether he plainly just wants to lean on your hands as support.

Compare the difference in the two scenarios below. The first sequence demonstrates how I am changing direction using only the reins. This clearly creates an uncomfortable imbalance which has a negative effect on the horse's head carriage, ultimately leading to inefficiency and distracting the horse from his actual job.

Now take a look at the second sequence below, where I am using a pelvic twist to steer the horse and applying the reins lightly as a secondary aid. It is quite clear which instruction interferes less with the horse's carriage and overall balance. I achieve the same result but the horse is comfortable, focussed, and ready for his next instruction.

TEAM CHAT

Picture once again the scenario of someone sitting on your shoulders whilst you are walking on an ice rink – you would likely much prefer an instruction of a twist of your passenger's pelvis than a pull in the mouth which would ultimately lead to an imbalance.

TURNING EFFICIENTLY *close and collect…*

Now, when riding a polo pony, one thing is for sure: you will never give the swing 100 percent focus and concentration if you are still preoccupied with staying on! Polo ponies are notorious for their stopping and turning ability at speed, so in the early stages it is essential that you find out how all of this feels in isolation without the added distraction of the mallet or the ball.

As with all techniques involving motion, it's best to start off slowly and move up the gears, never getting to the panic stage where the instinct is to 'grip on', and turn the technique into strength.

Repeat the exercise overleaf as often as possible until the horse is totally light at the front and producing a 180 degree turn by minimal pelvic twisting and whip tapping.

Remember, horses should never be forced to do anything, and the whip should be seen as a positive aid to encourage the horse to move away from the sound it makes on the leather work of a breast plate when tapping it. Once the horse executes all turning with pelvic and leg motion only, whip tapping can be dispensed with. Constant repetition of any exercise will refine the movement to such a sophisticated state that the instruction will be barely visible to the eye.

top tip

Ideally the reins should be introduced as a secondary device/aid to all the body techniques.

remember this? see pg 38...

As you become more proficient with the technique and increase the intensity of the turning and pace, success should be measured on how much the horse will do with minimal aids. As thighs become stronger, instructions from the pelvis become much more concise. This allows the rider to leave the horse's mouth free, resulting in maximum efficiency and sharper turning.

Exercise 2
TURNING WITH THE PELVIS

The first thing you will need for this exercise is a barrier, and this can be as obvious as a wall or a fence, or as simple as the boards around a pitch or even the white boundary line on the grass.

To begin, slide the feet out of the stirrups. Discard the mallet and hold the reins as normal in the left hand, taking a whip in the right hand, and holding it like a pen, positioning that hand above the horse's withers. Doing this will allow you to touch the horse on both the left and

right shoulder whilst keeping the right hand in a constant position. The whip should be seen as a positive aid to encourage the horse to move away from the sound it makes on the leather work of a breast plate when tapping it.

Proceed along a parallel line adjacent to the barrier in walk. Next, look directly over the shoulder closest to the barrier and fix your vision on a specific point behind you.

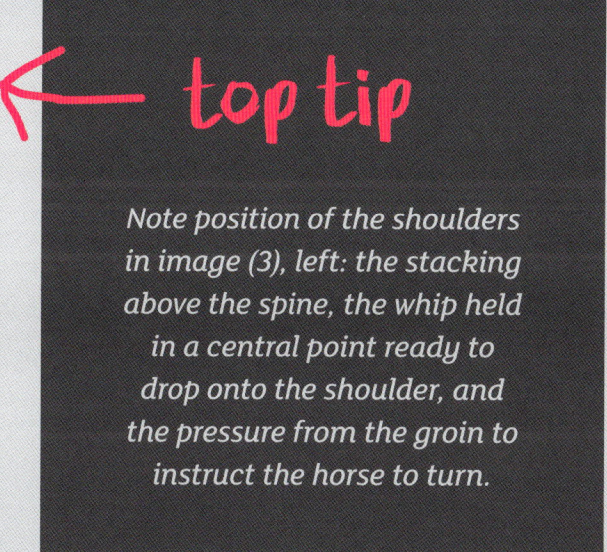

top tip

Note position of the shoulders in image (3), left: the stacking above the spine, the whip held in a central point ready to drop onto the shoulder, and the pressure from the groin to instruct the horse to turn.

Be careful that the horse does not stray from his parallel track next to the boundary whilst doing this. Do not make any turns yet but inform the horse that this is just the feeling he will receive when his rider is looking behind. Make the turn a couple of strides later by raising the reins to let him know that another instruction is coming.

Imagine there are two buttons on the saddle labelled left and right, situated just behind the pommel. Twist and push the button with the opposite groin to the direction of turn so that's right for a left turn and left for a right turn. Keep twisting until the horse has turned 180 degrees and faces the opposite direction without losing any rhythm or tempo - this will be easily achieved by gentle heel tapping.

Once happy with the sequence and having completed no more than say five strides, introduce a tapping on the opposite shoulder to the direction of turn. Vary the strides between each turn, say, three to five, and intensify the turning motion so that it becomes less of a semi-circle produced by the horse, and more of a skip as the hind legs stay anchored, acting as a pivot, and the horse brings his shoulders up and round to face the new direction.

Your lower legs will be regularly encouraging consistent impulsion, with heavy reliance on the thighs. After a couple of minutes, the muscles needing to be worked on and strengthened will be readily apparent, but also **the horse will have identified the feeling and the difference between his rider just looking behind and the instruction to turn.**

the essential things you're gonna need!

Basic Polo Riding

With the fundamentals for riding a horse in place, this chapter presents the overall theme of riding for polo – loose, effortless, fluent – as a foundation where you can achieve versatility. We are now going to identify how the basics of riding for polo are adapted for the purpose of hitting a ball and general playing:

01 Walk
02 Trot
03 Canter
04 Transitions

four fundamentals for fluency!

01/04 WALK (move like you mean it)

Polo is one of the fastest sports in the world, and so the whole theme of the riding element should be healthy, lively, positive, and energetic from the offset. Even to the untrained eye, you can spot a pro and an untrained beginner a mile off just by the way they sit on a horse. To become a pro you must aspire to look like one – which doesn't mean you need to grow your hair long, smoke Marlboro Lights, and mutter in Spanish, but it does include getting on and walking off! What it means is that you need to adopt the confident aura that is more likely to get you on the front cover of *Hello!* magazine instead of *Farmer's Weekly*!

I have to admit, slovenly walking is one of my all time 'pet hates'. It communicates a bad message to the horse and resembles nothing more than a frustrated adult dragging a sulky child around a shopping mall. So once you are mounted, be positive with aids. The frequency of several little taps with the heels is always far preferable to a booting in the ribs often accompanied by 'Yaaah!' whilst the horse still sets off at a snail's pace.

The walk is a four-time beat as each of the horse's legs has its own individual foot fall. At a bare minimum, good measure for tempo and rhythm should be no less than one foot fall per second, with occasional encouragement by tapping heels to create enthusiasm.

02/04 TROT

It never ceases to amaze me quite how much controversy there is about the trotting polo pony, but my instinct has always told me that it's a good thing. Aside from all the positive exercise and health reasons for trotting a polo pony, when it comes to the riding benefits and how it improves a player, it is one of **the** most beneficial gaits you can learn to master.

In addition to this, and to be totally blunt, nothing is quite as entertaining as watching a relatively new player heroically cantering off the pitch just as his horse breaks into trot and destroys almost all trace of sporting grace or elegance as the rider is clearly incapable of riding to one of the horse's most basic movements. Add to this visually painful image an audience of family, a great aunt, a bunch of society's most beautiful, and the majority of his work colleagues. **If this sounds uncomfortably familiar, then I suggest you learn to trot, and do it before your next match!**

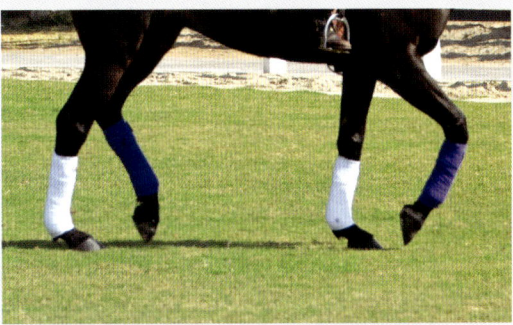

Now I know that traditionally polo is played at speed and rarely will you see horses trotting around on a polo pitch. However, learning to ride to the trot is guaranteed to produce a firm and secure balanced riding position due to the frequency of motion and the elevation it produces. Riding it correctly is of paramount importance to any aspiring player's progression.

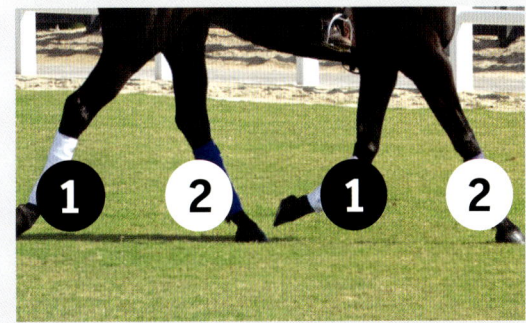

Trotting is a two-time movement that is produced when two diagonal hooves hit the ground synchronised at exactly the same time. This movement presents two options for classical riding: either sitting trot, or more traditionally, rising trot. In simple terms, in the first instance the rider remains sitting throughout the duration of the sequence, whilst in the latter the rider's position allows a rising out of the saddle on one of the beats, and a return back into the saddle for the following one and so on.

THE SITTING TROT

The technique used to develop good sitting trot is to firstly take the feet out of the stirrups – an act of fear and dread for many of my new students who have conveniently bypassed this stage in a bid to canter and reach the ball. It's worth noting that nearly all accomplished players will have had a wealth of experience from childhood involving

Initially, to the untrained rider, trotting without stirrups seems to be an exercise in painful self-preservation, but the true benefit lies in learning how to accommodate the 'violence' of the trot movement.

hours of pony club exercises trotting without stirrups (generally conducted by some hideous instructress who clearly had problems at home!). As a result they will have built up unique and specific riding muscles that no gym machine can ever develop. Commitment is needed to go through this stage if you are serious about wanting to improve your polo.

It really is a case of no pain, no gain, no game! The benefits, however, are incalculable. Initially, to the untrained rider, trotting without stirrups seems to be all about an exercise in painful self-preservation, but the true benefit lies in learning how to accommodate the 'violence' of the trot movement.

Using less deliberate strength and learning to adopt a much gentler approach will produce a lightness of movement. Done correctly, it will completely remove all potential bouncing at any pace as the body learns how to absorb motion in specific suspension points. The exercise will also produce those true 'riding muscles' generally only appreciated and located the day after a first hard lesson!

The trick to sitting trot is to understand what is happening. Bursting into trot activates the 'we're going to die!' part of the brain which in turn leads to a hunching of the back and a lean forwards – literally an effort to produce the foetal position. The reality is that the motion is directly below the centre of gravity. As a result, sitting on top of it – or worse still – leaning in front of it, is going to produce some painfully spectacular results! **All that is required is to tip backwards away from the vertical and the energy will be contained within the pelvis.**

no pain, no gain, no game!

THE RISING TROT

When you are capable of sitting trot, you can advance to the more traditionally used technique of rising trot. However, be aware that polo saddles are built primarily to play polo and hit out of, as opposed to ride in with an equestrian style. Unlike traditional general purpose equestrian saddles that have knee rolls, polo saddles lie flat against the horse. The upside is that they allow for the greatest freedom of movement and versatility; the downside is the absence of a barrier to stop the knees sliding too far forward and therefore unbalancing the body.

Polo saddles are constructed to accommodate a hitting position: the half seat and the specific absence of knee rolls allows for greater freedom of rider movement. As a result of their basic form, polo saddles demand a position from the rider that is both independent and truly balanced. Knee rolls on a general purpose saddle can mask imbalance, and whilst it could appear that a rider has control, the exercise on page 54 will show the riders amongst you just how reliant it is possible to become on the GP saddle construction for support.

Pushing away with the lower legs produces stability and strong thighs. The chest stays on a vertical which rises up from the horse's neck strap and encourages a correct hinging movement at the hips - different from using stirrups like climbing stairs and "falling" back into the saddle

Unlike traditional general purpose equestrian saddles that have knee rolls, polo saddles lie flat against the horse. The upside: they allow for greater freedom of movement and versatility. The downside: without them the knees can slide too far forward, which in turn will unbalance the body.

Polo saddles demand a position from the rider that is both independent and truly balanced. Knee rolls on a general purpose saddle can mask imbalance, and whilst it could appear that a rider has control, it is possible to become very reliant on the GP saddle construction for support.

Exercise 3
POWER TROTTING

Of all of the exercises you can ever do to produce upper leg, core, and thigh strength, **this is by far one of the more valuable ones**. The power trotting exercise must be completed in a figure of eight and ideally against a barrier or the boards at the side of a pitch perhaps.

To begin, establish a trot that is extremely rhythmical and almost breaking into canter, complete several circles approximately ten meters in diameter.

When you're ready, add a second circle and produce a pure figure of eight, changing the diagonal in the middle. Following a couple of warm-up circles in each direction, begin to lengthen or squash the circles, so from above, the image of the track you are riding is more like a very elongated figure of eight running parallel to the barrier, approximately three metres at its widest point.

During the course of this exercise, the horse's natural reaction is to either drop back down to walk or break into canter. The ability to keep the horse's speed constant throughout relies on an excellent hand (brakes) and leg (accelerator) relationship and a position where the rider's legs can hover around close to the accelerator. The result of this is that there is no opportunity now to stand on the stirrups, so it forces a highly developed position that is almost independent of stirrups.

It is at the turning points that most benefits are achieved as the horse is required to maintain the fast rhythm and tempo.

After only a couple of minutes spent on this exercise, both participants will need a rest, but it will highlight the amount of work needed to develop upper thigh strength.

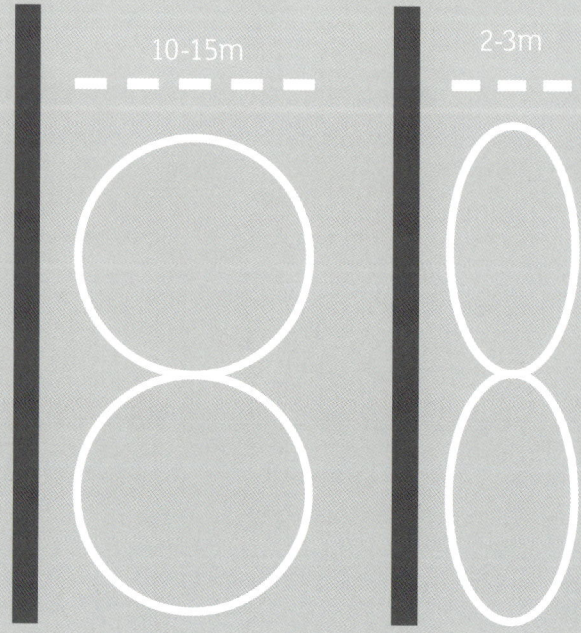

the key to success is maintaining good rhythm and tempo!

TEAM CHAT

Of all of the training routines you can do to produce upper leg, core, and thigh strength, the exercise on the opposite page is by far one of the most valuable. The key to success lies in maintaining rhythm and tempo whilst executing a fast rising trot in very tight circles. An additional plus point is how supple and flexible the horse becomes, as to complete the exercise successfully his hind legs will collect further and further underneath, producing much more power for acceleration.

> A polo player must firstly be a great rider and secondly a great hitter.

03/04 CANTER — *now the real fun can begin!*

Canter: the gait most people associate with polo and of course ultimately galloping.

Done correctly, canter is the pace where riding seems effortless – total harmony with the horse, whose movement will be uncompromised by the weight of a rider. Done badly? Painful, ugly, and abusive to both participants, and in the case of the rider's prowess – slightly humorous to watch!

The canter is a three-time movement when two of the horse's hooves touch the ground at the same time, therefore acting as one, followed by the other two separately, hence a three-time beat.

THE CANTER SEQUENCE

A horse standing still going straight into canter begins with a hind leg first, then the two diagonal legs acting as one, with the remaining foreleg finishing the sequence. The chosen hind leg that started the sequence ultimately determines which of the front legs becomes 'the leading leg'.

In the sequence to the right, you can clearly identify the sequence of foot falls by the coloured bandages:

Blue starts the sequence (1), followed by the two reds together (2), and finally the white (3). The sequence then starts again.

blue, red, white!

A horse standing still going straight into canter begins with a hind leg first, then the two diagonal legs acting as one, with the remaining foreleg finishing the sequence. The chosen hind leg that started the sequence ultimately determines which of the front legs becomes 'the leading leg'.

As we've discussed, the theme of all riding for polo is versatility and adopting a position that's non saddle dependent. The canter is a smooth flowing motion and riders can expect to feel a circular motion with the pelvis throughout the sequence as the horse completes each stride.

Based on what you will shortly be required to do in the saddle to allow you to hit the ball, it is essential at this point to learn how to ride loosely without gripping the saddle unnecessarily with your thighs.

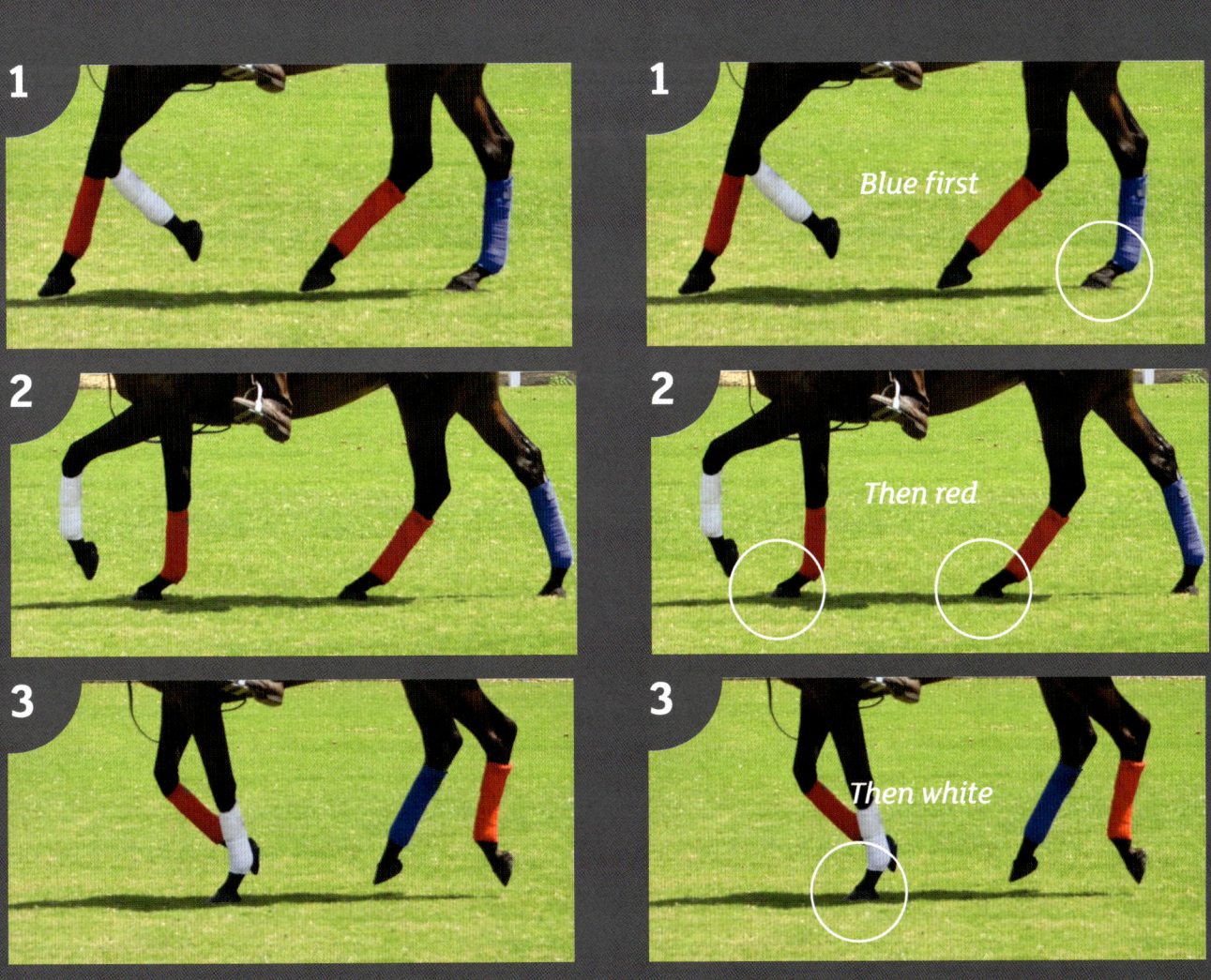

remember this?

The best way to achieve this is to ask the horse for canter (remembering the accelerator is way further back than one would normally appreciate). Once the first stride is achieved, bring the shoulders back behind 'the vertical' (as we have just discussed in the trot section: all bouncing happens when a rider is directly on top of the motion), so the trick in this case is to **tilt the body backwards about five inches away from the centre of gravity**. This position creates a new channel for concussion down through the legs to the knees and final expulsion through the ankles as they gently push up and down against the stirrups with each stride – the trick is to **rest** the feet in the stirrups so the heels become suspension points.

top tip

This technique of being 'carried' by the horse, rather than a more traditional 'drive' of the horse forward with your back and seat, will ultimately allow for many of the bodily twisting and turning requirements of hitting.

TEAM CHAT

All the techniques highlighted so far are for non-hitting positions. They are designed to train the body to accept motion and movement with an overall theme of versatility. This ensures that the underlying riding foundation is fluid rather than strong. When it comes to hitting the ball, a much more exact position is required: **the half seat**, which will be covered in detail in the next chapter.

Tilt the body backwards so the energy is released through the heels

This technique of being 'carried' by the horse rather than a more traditional 'drive' of the horse forward with your back and seat, will ultimately allow for the versatility needed for many of the bodily twisting and turning requirements of hitting.

04/04 TRANSITIONS

Unlike conventional riding where some disciplines require a very fixed position and the rider's job is to use the seat to 'drive a horse forward', polo often requires the rider to separate upper and lower body – neither of which should be reliant on the other, but occasionally work as a counterbalance.

Experienced riders have the ability to channel energy through their bodies and absorb concussion. Without this technique the rider will be subject to ALL of the horse's motion which understandably is not desirable on the approach to a ball! Below is a great exercise to train the pelvis to absorb concussion.

Exercise 4
TROT TO CANTER TRANSITIONS

Ride forward on a straight line or a circle collecting the horse up to canter. After only a couple of strides, raise the reins and the pelvis and come back to trot. Remember to keep the rib cage high at all times.

In essence, the pelvis in canter is following a circular motion which flows horizontally, whilst the trot motion flows diagonally upwards with a much more intense elevation. Every three to five strides repeat: trot to canter, canter to trot.

The trick in executing this exercise perfectly is to master the art of pelvic versatility which will allow you to accommodate the transitions up and down smoothly and effortlessly.

Remember: your ultimate goal is to hit the ball, which will never happen if you are constantly subject to the horse's motion.

this exercise creates flexibility!

CHAPTER CHECKLIST

All I have hoped to achieve in this chapter is to try to educate the less experienced riders and create some empathy and compassion for the horse in the pure golden rules. If I have imparted even the smallest consideration for the 'mechanics' of the horse, you are certainly one positive step forward, and have laid the very first foundation layer from which to build your riding and hitting skills.

You should now be able to:

- ✓ Balance correctly

- ✓ Accommodate forward motion

- ✓ Stop the horse with the body

- ✓ Steer the horse with the body

- ✓ Produce an energised walk

- ✓ Perform sitting and rising trot

- ✓ Power trot in a figure of eight

- ✓ Ride fluidly at a canter

- ✓ Accommodate trot-to-canter transitions

Advanced Polo Riding

This chapter highlights those areas where and when you do need to apply strength, and highlights the muscles, techniques, and exercises you will need to develop that strength if and when required. It also addresses how the basic fundamentals of horse riding are adapted for the purposes of playing polo.

Once you have all of the basic skills in place, you should really try to take time out to practice them in isolation. Training this way will allow you to perfect each component part, and then you just need to put them all together. Polo riding is about fluidity and about gliding between one riding situation and the next with the confidence of knowing that if a situation requires you to hold strong, you have acquired the muscles to do it.

The techniques over the following pages are designed to help you develop specific polo riding muscles and aid stability. These are:

01 The Half Seat
02 Acceleration and Deceleration
03 Efficient Turning
04 Changing Direction
05 Versatility
06 The Tube

six steps to success!

01/06 THE HALF SEAT

riding position for hitting the balls! (and ultimate horse control)

A half seat is purely designed to enable you to bring the shoulders in front of the pelvis to allow maximum rotation of the upper body. It consequently produces a series of angles from the hips through to knees and ankles that will absorb the concussion of the horse's movement.

A good half seat will allow you to constantly flow parallel with the ground regardless of the horse's gait because these angles absorb the motion, almost as if you are riding on a monorail. Inconsistent or badly produced half seats will often result in a too high torso position and a standing in the stirrups which just means you are subject to all of the horse's movement. This would be like trying to hit a golf ball out of a helicopter on a very windy day!

The Classic Half Seat
The angle at the back of the knee, the heels down, and the soles of the feet pushing away, together create the essential suspension points.

all of this weight...

...is resting inside the knee against the saddle

Adhering to the two golden rules of shoulders and chest in front of pelvis, and suspension on the knees and ankles, the trick in developing your own personal half seat is to know where 'home' is. By this I mean that in the chaos of a game it would make sense that you would ideally need to have muscle memory and positions that feel familiar, so you know when you've 'arrived'.

Tearing around the pitch on a speeding horse will inevitably push you higher out of the saddle, so on the approach to the ball you need to be well settled in your half seat – as this is how you would have trained and most of your hand-to-eye coordination will be based on this specific position.

The shots above demonstrate three different examples of players adopting a half seat, adhering to all the golden rules but all with a different and varied style, based on their unique and individual body make-up.

The important point to remember from now on is that **every rider is built differently.** Some tall people may have short legs and a long torso, others the complete opposite, so **how one individual produces a half seat will differ from the next.**

Exercise 5

THE HALF SEAT

Perform this exercise when the horse is standing still to allow you to make adjustments.

1) From where you are sitting in a normal relaxed position, slide the whole body back about five inches to create a space under your crotch. In some cases you may even need to sit on the cantle (the back of the saddle).

2) Once you have done this, fold the upper body forward and effectively kneel down on the horse. Then allow all of the upper body weight to rest on the inside of the thighs and most importantly sink down as deep as possible onto the knees – **there now should be no daylight between the crotch, thighs, and saddle.**

3) Now lift the chin up and open wide at the chest to create the essential arch in the lower back.

Once all of this is in place, you may now push hard down with the heels, and then away laterally from the horse with the inside ball of the foot, almost turning your toes into a central point in front of the horse's nose. For those of you who ski, this position is not unlike a snow plough.

Viewed from the front, this position is very much pyramid-shaped, starting with the head and widening all the way down to the base at the feet below. In addition, it will appear that there is almost no flat platform to stand on; instead, the feet are positioned almost as if pushing against the sides of a small tunnel wall.

As soon as the horse moves at any pace, the rider's backside will remain at a constant height from the saddle because the angles will now absorb the concussion of the horse's movement.

practice this exercise regularly for half seat mastery!

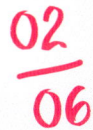 ## ACCELERATION AND DECELERATION

Polo ponies are renowned for being able to stop and turn on a sixpence. The reality is, however, that there is rarely a need to stop a polo pony completely during a game. That would be the same as arriving at a junction in a car, turning the engine off, and taking it out of gear. Think of the effort needed to turn it back on, put it into gear, and driving off again! The direction of play changes rapidly and frequently during a game, and the trick is to master how to instruct the pony to accelerate and decelerate with minimum aids, allowing him to remain efficient.

In a previous section, we looked at how just a simple movement in front or behind 'the vertical' was sufficient to make the pony go or stop. Now we just need to elaborate on this basic principle and the best way to learn this technique is actually back in trot so that initially the momentum is easy to cope with. I regularly perform the exercise outlined in this chapter on my young horses as it creates exceptional lightness in the mouth and really gets them to listen to my body movements. **I pretend that the reins are actually made of small thin pieces of cotton that would snap if I pulled too much. This just helps focus on really using the body to control the horse and never your own strength.**

Exercise 6
ACCELERATE / DECELERATE

Begin by establishing a healthy forward-going rising trot and adopt a half seat with quite a low chest position so that the change in position will be obvious to the horse.

Lift the chest almost back onto the vertical which will allow the weight to flow through the heels, but remain in a half seat with the bottom out of the saddle. At the same time, raise the hands **vertically**, keeping a light but firm contact with the horse's mouth. Push hard down with the heels. As soon as there is a feeling of deceleration, fold back down to the low-chested half seat position again and encourage the trot back up to its original speed.

Repeat this exercise as often as required, ensuring that the movement of raising hands and pushing through heels are both very obvious to the horse.

Try to avoid a hurried, panicked motion as you accelerate, just waiting for him to collect himself and push forward. It won't be very long before a simple lift of the hands

Accelerate

Decelerate

Remember, the horse FEELS everything, so a matter of five inches in front and then back to the vertical will be obvious enough for him to feel the weight shift.

this exercise teaches application of technique over strength

and chest is all that is required for him to slow down instantly as he feels the reins stroke him up his neck, and relaxing back into a half seat is enough to suggest that he accelerate forward. Once this is completed consistently in trot, try in canter.

Be aware that initially the horse may wish to balance himself on the rider's hands, but if they are kept still as they are raised he should collect himself up behind. It's also important to make sure that the reins are not pulled back or he is actually physically stopped at any point. Just lift and decelerate, collapse forward and accelerate.

Work on a rectangular-shaped track about ten metres in length. Accelerate quickly down the long sides and decelerate just before you enter the short sides. Here is where the circles are introduced. As the horse becomes more efficient, intensify the exercise by reducing the stopping distance. For example, instead of taking five strides to go from fast to slow, make it happen in three.

Collected canter
Three canter strides
2.7-3.3m per stride

5m

Extended canter 10m

STOPPING AT SPEED

Having taught for over 20 years, the lack of understanding of horse mechanics amongst players – even at the top level – still concerns me. As polo has evolved, there is a distinct obsession that to get a polo pony to stop at any speed you must make it 'sit down'. Well, let's just think about it: a horse cannot stop in the air, so violently pulling its head up and back only leaves two feet on the ground, and yet perhaps in our enthusiasm to get to the ball or make a play we seem to forget it has four legs to make the job easier and more efficient.

To understand this completely, you would need to observe its true mechanics without human interference. We've touched on the natural horse stopping and turning abruptly away from a fence scenario, and by watching this we can witness the pure efficiency that horses possess and the specific way in which an individual animal wants to function.

Generally what a horse actually wants to do when stopping or turning is true enough 'sit down', but he wants to lower his shoulders too to get his centre of gravity lower. He also wants to arch his back to absorb and reverse the forward state of motion and extend and drop his head and neck to balance the whole process.

However, despite all of these requirements to produce efficiency, all too often you will see players pulling the head up and back – the total opposite of how the horse wants to operate. If you've ever ridden a horse that is strong, when asking for a stop you might just question for a second – is he not just fighting to do what you asked him to do in the first place and did you actually give him a chance to do what you asked?

here it is again from pg 38

As polo 'people' we are self-proclaiming animal lovers... but when was the last time we ever did something to our labrador dog to produce an expression like the above?

This image is unfortunately an all too common sight on polo pitches around the world... but just look how differently the horse operates without interference. Remember the below from page 19?

03/06 EFFICIENT TURNING

As we've already discussed, we are aspiring to allow the horse to remain efficient, which is only possible when you don't interfere with his own natural way of doing things. **Therefore you need to use the groin and the pelvis as the steering wheel and the reins as a secondary aid.**

remember this?

The extent a horse turns will be dependent on the extent the pelvis is rotated, and the exercise on the opposite page allows you to locate exactly which muscles we need to be using. As with all circle work, it is vital to change the rein and direction frequently to avoid developing rider or horse too much on one side. And as with all training and muscle building, if you want to get real value for your efforts and good development, you will need go to the point of human exhaustion, rest for a couple of minutes and begin again.

It is exactly like working out at the gym. Ultimately, the harder you work and the more you put in, the bigger and better the result.

sets + reps + constant repetition

Exercise 7
CIRCLES WITHIN CIRCLES

this exercise creates the ultimate core and inner thigh and leg strength!

In this exercise, we shall be creating circles within circles, all without the use of stirrups. Firstly, establish a healthy rhythmical canter clockwise on a ten metre circle. Be aware where the centre of the circle is to encourage consistency, and we can also use it as our opposite boundary.

Every five strides or so, lift the rib cage and the reins, twisting the pelvis to the right, and produce a smaller inner circle no further than the centre of the main one we have just formed.

Be conscious of using the reins as a secondary command to the horse and try as much as possible to make him turn by stacking the shoulders parallel above his spine and twisting the pelvis continuously until the circle is complete and you are back where we started on the main outer circle.

CHANGING DIRECTION

04/06

Flying changes or changing leading legs are the terms used to describe the horse's movement when it changes its leg sequence in the middle of a stride. Horses do this most commonly when changing direction, however they are also able to produce a flying change in a straight line without any interference with rhythm or tempo.

A horse's correct leg sequence will ensure absolute efficiency, especially when turning, so it is vitally important as players that we know how to execute this movement even in the early stages of learning. Remember, when you are riding, all you are doing is trying to capture the way the horse does things naturally, harness those actions and then just ask him to do things on command.

The trick to achieving all of this is to firstly be clear with your instruction. Make sure it's an instruction he understands and then leave him alone to get on with it!

'Gliding' is a great word for describing the execution of a flying change with a forward and continuous state of motion. If the horse was running free around a field and wanted to change direction he would happily and simply just change his leg sequence.

top tip →

This movement goes wrong usually because the horse is distracted by the rider's interference. Remember, he already knows how to do it and would prefer to do it in a flowing manner; it is up to us as riders to let him!

The PELVIS is the steering wheel

top tip

It will certainly come as a surprise to some how early on I teach flying changes to beginners, but they really are not as difficult or complicated as some will make out – just follow the rules. I need to reiterate that ANY horse knows how to complete a flying change, so this following exercise is to teach a rider how and when to ask for it.

The key thing to remember is that **the pelvis really IS the steering wheel**. That way you'll be discouraged from wrestling with his mouth to force the change or leaning, forcing him to stagger into a change. Learning to accomplish a flying change is much easier on the back of an experienced horse who is exceptional with his execution – basically so you know and understand what it feels like.

Exercise 8
CHANGING DIRECTION

Begin by laying out polo bandages into a shape similar to the one shown below. The corridor between the two semi-circles and the exits need to be large enough to accommodate a polo pony (about three metres wide). The trick is to gather the horse up into quite a fast canter and to be disciplined in **fixing your shoulders and hips together**.

On the curved approach, the shoulders and hips will be rotated approximately 45 degrees as you enter the grid. Once in the central corridor, the shoulders and hips will be momentarily square onto the horse, then on the completion of his next stride twist the pelvis and shoulders to face a 45-degree angle left or right and hold the position still.

NEVER lean in the new direction, only twist and keep the weight equal in both heels. The bandages on the floor will encourage the horse to follow the boundary line. Regardless of whether the horse changed his sequence or not, continue to circle round, maintaining rhythm and tempo, and enter again using the same technique.

Don't forget, a horse travelling on a straight line who then chooses to change direction

WILL change his own legs – the trick for the rider is to master the skill of the twist at exactly the right time of his stride sequence.

With enough repetition, most horses will change fluidly every time – it is the rider's responsibility to ensure that instruction to him is consistent. As progress is made, the physical grid can of course be dispensed with, and attempts made to change the lead leg in an open space. Only when all the executions are correct can you begin to make the circles smaller and more intense, but always be listening and feeling for the rhythm and tempo of the stride.. 123... 123... change... 123... 123... and so on..

It is important to note that throughout this explanation there has been no mention of using reins - and that is for a very specific reason: the quieter the rider becomes on a horse and the less 'noise' and movement, the more sensitive he becomes. As the pelvis is now the steering wheel, the reins literally touching him on his neck are a secondary device to confirm that yes, this twist of the pelvis does in fact mean change your direction, Mr. Horse!

Remember:
He doesn't want us to interfere with his bodily mechanics, he just wants to know what it is we want him to do.

Pelvis and shoulders twist to the right

Pelvis and shoulders twist to the left

05/06

VERSATILITY

In basic principle, when it comes to hitting, the more momentum you can create with the mallet, the further the ball will travel. A simple enough statement, but to do that, you need to have the ability to take the stick head as far away from the ball as possible. **General hitting inconsistency or other problems are rarely with the arm and the mallet, but often with an insufficiently balanced foundation down below to support the hitting structure as it grows higher.**

really important!

Throughout this book, there is a phrase that appears more than any other: **versatility in the saddle**. In order to ride effectively, hit correctly, and maximise on all of the playing opportunities, you MUST be versatile in the saddle. This ability depends on the technique adopted using the stirrups and saddle to support the upper body.

It is only possible to achieve true versatility when the thighs and lower legs are positioned behind you, and all of the upper body weight is supported by the thighs, which must be positioned behind an imaginary line dropped vertically from the chest.

use the exercise on the next page to create versatility and stability!

It is only possible to achieve true versatility when the thighs and lower legs are positioned behind you, and all of the upper body weight is supported by the thighs, which must be positioned behind an imaginary line dropped vertically from the chest.

The next stage of producing versatility is to adopt a technique of using pressure in the heels against the stirrups to strengthen the relationship between the heel and groin. Without this technique, you will always be restricted on all-round vision and the ability to reach for the big shots. It's all about being versatile enough to accommodate the upper body weight from one side to the other and on to the knees.

Exercise 9
SINK LEFT, SINK RIGHT

— understand it —

Begin this exercise by sitting normally in a chair (with the back behind you and legs forward) and try to look over your shoulder. Sitting on your backside with the thighs in front immediately presents a restricted position, **but when you turn the chair around to allow the chest to come forward, the arm is able to extend higher behind as the pelvis is now versatile.** If you then move your legs back behind you to allow the collapse of the pelvis forward, the results are instant and present an opportunity for all round vision.

Equally important to note is what is happening to the knees and how low you are able to sink as you rotate left and right. In my experience, this is not a technique that necessarily comes naturally as polo saddles will automatically force you into an 'armchair' type of position as soon as you are mounted. It needs to be understood and practiced.

— apply it —

In order to produce this movement, position yourself ready for the rotation and then as you twist, aim to get your chest facing completely to the left and again to the right. When you attempt this on a horse, try it out in all paces and practice sinking as low as you possibly can onto the knee opposite to the way you are turning. The trick to remaining balanced is to line up your shoulders each time you rotate to a position directly above the horse's spine. Not only will this skill allow you to have all-round vision, it will develop the relationship between the groin and heel, which, as you read on, is absolutely essential for hitting.

In the example on the opposite page, note the depth of how much the knees need to sink to allow for full body rotation. The trick to remaining balanced is to line up the shoulders each time you rotate to a position above the horse's spine. Focus should be placed on developing the groin-to-heel relationship to give you the stability.

Lift lower leg and sink to right knee, pushing hard against right heel

Lift lower leg and sink to left knee, pushing hard against left heel

The degree of stability that you are able to achieve with the groin-to-heel technique is absolutely critical in determining the number of planes you will ultimately be able to find.

06/06 THE TUBE

I hope it is becoming more apparent that the methodology I use is to first produce and practice all of the body balancing techniques in isolation on the horse and then apply the polo mallet to the body. So it is at this riding stage you also need to master the art of remaining balanced whilst looking straight down at the ball. The ability to place the chin on the chest is right up there in the top five fundamentals of successful hitting. I purposely introduce this technique at this stage because vision is completely linked to the balancing process.

It is almost impossible to miss the ball if the line of sight is directly over it because the shoulder rotation makes the arm swing directly through it. A good technique is to imagine that the ball is at the bottom of a long tube like a drain pipe reaching up from the ground to a point roughly level with the rider's collarbone.

Your line of sight is perpendicular to your face…

Whilst it may appear here that I'm looking at the ball, my actual line of site is still 45 degrees…

Only by physically placing my chin on my chest will I achieve a true perpendicular line of sight

top tip

For many new riders it is quite unnerving to try to produce this 'chin on the chest position' as they are often really reluctant to look away from the direction of motion. So best to get it sorted and out of the way and totally ingrained into the muscle memory. More often than not, a correct head position and line of vision will be the difference between a hit or a miss.

In a normal standing position facing forward, the line of sight is 90 percent to the face. To look down at the feet means lowering the chin to the chest by tipping the head. Without it, there would be a strange and awkward peering over the nose. The vision requirement to hit a ball correctly is to have the line of sight directly over the ball without disrupting the 90-degree norm, and therefore the only way to achieve this is indeed to put the chin on the chest – initially not a pleasant sensation when you are just learning to ride!

Very often in an effort to get the line of sight correct, a novice player will instinctively work in reverse and try to bring his chest to his chin by leaning out as he attempts to position his line of sight over the ball. The problem in this case is that in order to achieve this the player absolutely HAS to stand in the right stirrup and **lean**.

Standing produces two detrimental effects: firstly, the player is now subject to the horse's movement; and secondly, to stop the horse staggering to the right, the player now has another job in forcing the reins left to compensate for the lean. Why give yourself an unnecessary extra job when the focus now should really be on hitting the ball. Plus, it is much easier to hit a ball dealing with just one overall theme – of fluidity and fluency – rather than unsettling the horse with half of the body strong and the other half attempting to be fluid and fluent on the swing.

TEAM CHAT

Back to a car analogy, if we take the engine starter motor out - in relation to the whole engine it is a pretty small part – but if it's missing, nothing will work. Equally, the small action of placing the chin on the chest is fundamental if the 'hitting machine' is going to function with maximum effectiveness.

examples of tubes

It is almost impossible to miss the ball if the line of sight is directly over it because the technique of rotating the shoulders back to hit makes the arm swing directly through it. A good technique is to imagine that the ball is at the bottom of a long tube, like a drain pipe, reaching up from the ground to a point roughly level with the rider's collarbone.

Exercise 10
CHIN ON CHEST

On the approach to the ball using the muscles at the back of the neck and **not** leaning the chest over the ball, simply place the chin on the chest. This is actually easier said than done, so as a checkpoint, imagine making the top of the tube watertight with the whole of the face (as seen in example 1 below). The weight of the upper body will at this point still be above the horse and the line of sight will be directly over the ball.

When it comes eventually to applying the swing to the riding, the focus must be on keeping the head, and ultimately line of sight, in this position until the swinging right shoulder pushes the chin upwards as it continues along its course to its final destination (as seen in example 2 below).

work the tube!

Look straight down the tube...

...into the space the ball was in even after you hit it. Wait for the shoulder to lift the chin once it's achieved full extension on its upward motion.

CHAPTER CHECKLIST

You should now be able to:

 Produce a well-balanced half seat

 Accelerate and decelerate with a body movement more than reins

 Canter circles within circles using the pelvis and minimal reins

 Execute flying changes

 Have the ability to 'sink left / right' on the horse at all paces

 Ride at any pace with the ability to place the chin on the chest for a count of 1.5 seconds

PART II: ~~HITTING~~ winning ~~SUCCESSFULLY~~ at swinging

I say old chap, is that Lady Penelope trying to mount our pro?

swinging the Mallet ~~Essentials~~

THE IMPORTANCE OF FULLY UNDERSTANDING THE ESSENTIALS THAT MAKE UP A SWING

This chapter is broken down into five practical sections:

01 The Grip
02 The Pendulum
03 The Plane
04 The Shots
05 Intention

five top techniques to hit like a pro!

01/05 THE GRIP

Margin for error in the grip department is huge and as a young beginner player once myself, I certainly underestimated its importance and the effect it had on the early years of my playing career. Frustrated beyond belief with my hitting ability and consistency, I stripped, pushed, pulled, dissected, dismantled, and rebuilt my swing several times over. Only when I had come to my wit's end did I stop to question that inconsistency could actually be coming from the way I was holding the mallet.

So let's avoid all the pain – learning the optimum personal grip (and it is very personal) just requires a basic measuring technique: Begin by producing a half seat and allow the mallet to hang vertically from the shoulder. Reduce the height of the half seat by folding at the waist and bending the knees until the mallet head reaches the floor. This is YOUR contact position which is specific to you. It is based on the length of your torso on the horse. The mallet head should be perpendicular to the horse and this is now the perfect point of contact.

Resting the handle of the mallet against the flat of the palm, open the fingers as wide as they will go and begin to wrap them around the handle one by one, little finger first, ring finger, middle finger, index finger then thumb. **The fingers should be relaxed and the feeling should be that of encasing the handle and not squeezing it. There should be a slight 'V' shape between the index finger and thumb and the top crease of the forefinger should be just wrapping around the back of the thin end of the handle. This is *your* perfect grip.**

Any variation from this will have a negative effect on hitting. To prove the point, from this relaxed grip start to squeeze the handle and make a fist by closing the fingers together and have a look at the effect it has on the projection of the mallet from the arm. Open the fingers again and let it drop – it's obvious how much the grip needs to be relaxed with the fingers spread in order to achieve a true extension line from shoulder socket down to stick head, allowing the cigar shape to rest exactly parallel with the ground.

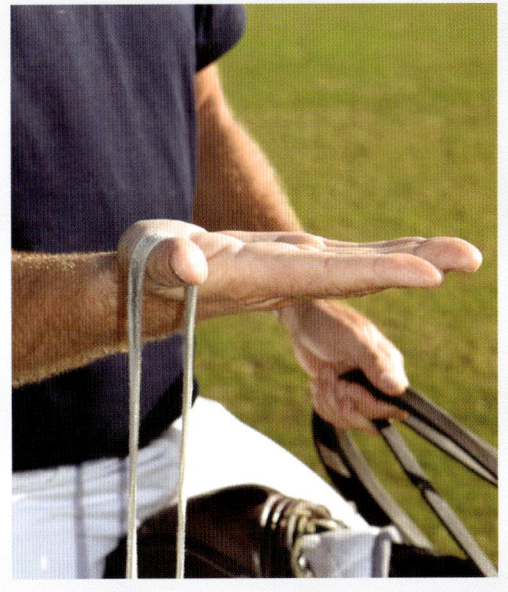

Once the grip has been accomplished, lift it to a vertical position in front and opposite the shoulder, and bend it back slightly towards you. This will allow identification of the exact balance points at the base of the index finger, in the wrist and in the elbow where the weight of the mallet is accommodated rather than it being supported with strong fingers. When the mallet is vertical and perfectly balanced, all the weight will be travelling straight down the cane and directly to the floor.

Now that you know how it should feel, you can apply the sling. Start with the palm facing up. Place the sling over the thumb and rotate the hand anticlockwise so the sling rests on the back of the hand below the knuckles. Depending on the size of your hand, you may need to use several twists to help with balance and support – a good measure on how tight is to apply as many twists as required, so when the fingers are open you will be able to balance the mallet vertically on the base of the index finger.

Exercise 11
BALANCING THE MALLET

As an exercise, begin to move the mallet around the body to the furthest points around the horse as far as reach allows, pushing and pulling forwards, backwards and sideways without going much higher than the shoulder.

All mallet movement should be via the shoulder socket, elbow, and chest, and never the forearm. The test at this stage is if a glass of water was balanced on top of the mallet head, would you spill any as it moved from one point to the next?

top tip

1

2

Repeat until perfect balance is achieved with the mallet as it is rotated to all points around the horse. This exercise produces the feeling of how to work the mallet with the body **by using the chest and shoulder framework together in conjunction with the pelvis.**

02/05 THE PENDULUM

this is central to producing a balanced + effective swing

When it comes to hitting the ball and to fully understand a shot, let's strip the swing back to its most primitive form. The intellectuals amongst you will understand the term "centrifugal force": a brief description being an energy force created from a central point, in this case the shoulder. You can feel the energy if you swing a complete revolution and the stick starts to slide out of the hand.

The second sensation you get is that of the momentum created as a result of a pendulum. All shots contain pendulums. Pendulums are exact things – they have two equal visible sides at either side of contact; they have two moments of suspension, an area of acceleration and an equal area of deceleration. The inability to produce a pendulum within the structure of a swing will account for the majority of hitting problems.

> **All shots contain pendulums. Pendulums are exact things – they have two equal visible sides at either side of contact; they have two moments of suspension, an area of acceleration and an equal area of deceleration.**

Pendulums are at the core of every balanced swing and can also be seen in pre-swings on the approach to a penalty shot. In this instance the player will use a pendulum to establish momentum whilst feeling for the moments of suspension and the areas of acceleration and deceleration because it will help to produce a correctly timed and balanced swing.

It's a really worthwhile exercise to swing giant pendulums as a warm up pre-hitting as a reminder of the feelings and characteristics you are ultimately wanting to produce. The larger the pendulum the more obvious the feelings are. Great examples are a child's swing or the 'pirate ship' ride at the fairground – by visualising, you can perhaps recall the weightlessness felt at the top on either side and the whoosh of acceleration as it swings to the bottom before decelerating to a moment of suspension at the top on the opposite side and the sequence begins again.

A PURE PENDULUM

Start with the left groin touching the saddle and chest facing right; finish with the right groin touching and chest facing left. The pelvis should be effectively fixed with the shoulders and move together as one.

true pendulums produce mirror images either side of contact

It is **this** feeling that a good player aspires to experience with **all** hitting. Problems occur when the swing actually gets smaller because it is harder to identify true pendulum characteristics. Children do not have adult strength, so when you watch them play, they swing the mallet as if it's a brick on a string. Assuming they lined up the horse correctly, their results are successful – by default, they swing a perfect pendulum.

Now that you know that pendulums are at the very heart of all hitting, and it is a pendulum that you should be aspiring to, you need to look at what the body needs to do to accommodate one.

Remember, a complete pendulum has two equal halves either side of contact. This means that when a player swings backwards to his furthest or chosen point he will need to accommodate the upper body movement with an almost identical movement with the pelvis. **From this moment onwards his pelvis will be effectively fixed with his shoulders and move together as one.** This will of course have an absolute effect on the rest of the body. Firstly, his chest will be facing to the right when the stick is behind, and if he is dealing with a true pendulum, when the shot is complete, his chest will be facing to the left. This essential requirement to clearly produce a pure and complete pendulum has come as a revelation to many players I have met who are experiencing hitting problems. Their pendulums were just never complete.

> **The essential requirement to clearly produce a pure and complete pendulum has come as a revelation to many players I have met who are experiencing hitting problems. Their pendulums were just never complete.**

Now, understandably there will of course be sceptics to this "phenomenon" who will have witnessed players swinging and finishing with their shoulders square on to the horse - and their eyes didn't deceive them, they are absolutely right, they did finish shoulders square. Why? It is likely that the instinct to hit the ball harder was too much to resist – the consequence being that the mallet is travelling so fast that

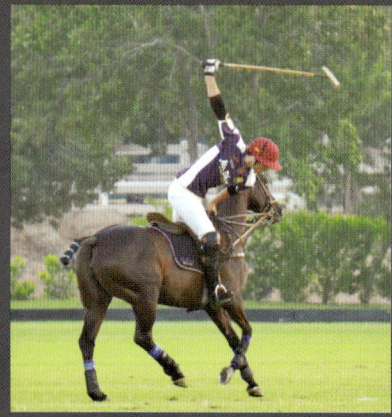

In this sequence, note the position of the player's chest facing to the right when he begins the shot, and on completion an almost mirror image of how he began, with his chest facing to the left.

Here is an example of a player starting with his chest to the right, but CHOOSING to finish chest square to absorb the power of the pendulum.

if the player didn't pull it back immediately after contact, assuming a square shoulder position, he would end up getting dragged off due to its speed. But more common with professional players is that the player deliberately cut the pendulum short. Why? Well to answer this needs acceptance of just how powerful a polo mallet pendulum actually is.

Take a very basic scenario of the arm pointing behind you at a ten o'clock position and with the stick 90 degrees at the wrist. Now swing a pendulum through a ball and finish at the two o'clock position. For anyone, young, old, male, female, tall or short, that ball will travel 30–40 yards without the introduction or creation of more energy. So quite simply for many, the most basic shot is too powerful to use. If your teammate for example is only 20 yards in front, the shot to use **is** a pendulum but some of its power needs to be absorbed by deliberately cutting it short.

This theory and application of using a complete pendulum as part of their technique has changed the playing life of hundreds of people I have taught. If there are hitting problems I strongly recommend

Finishing shots as a mirror-image of how they began.

a careful study of the swing and see how complete the internal pendulum is. Only when the shot is put under the microscope will the crime of surrendering to the instinct of hitting harder and faster be revealed.

At each moment of suspension, if a photo was taken of a player swinging on either side of the horse and his head was removed from the image, would it be possible to tell if he is beginning a forehand or ending a backhand, and equally the same on the other side?

To help reinforce this necessary requirement to produce a pendulum consisting of two equal sides, it should now make sense that at each moment of suspension, if a photo was taken of a player swinging on either side of the horse – and his head was removed from the image – it should not be possible to tell if he is beginning a forehand or ending a backhand, and equally the same on the other side.

Question:
Is this an image of the beginning of an off-side forehand or the end of a straight backhand?

The reason why it's not possible is because structurally they are the same shot in reverse and therefore will appear identical on both sides. So, applying this theory when swinging, you should aspire to produce an accurate mirror image of the body and stick position on completion of the swing, one which is identical to how it began.

THE PLANE

The next essential thing you will need to hit the ball is knowing where and how to find and establish the plane. The sheer nature of playing polo means that the game is fuelled with adrenalin, emotion, chaos, and imperfect hitting environments. Having the mental discipline to cope with these pressured situations is one requirement, but having subconscious muscle memory of where to begin shots is another.

Anyone walking in a straight line would not consciously go through a detailed thought process of 'lift knee, extend leg, body weight forward, heels down'. Equally, good players instinctively know where to begin shots that successfully send the ball in the direction they wish it to travel. When the stick is swung, it travels in a constant motion through the ball without faltering from its course.

The easiest way to understand the concept of a plane is to imagine that as soon as you point the mallet head in the direction you wish the ball to travel, two sheets of glass appear, sandwiching the mallet head and guiding the swing to and through the ball in the direction that was originally established – the same feeling you'd get as if swinging a brick on a piece of rope. The space the brick and rope occupy is flat and two-dimensional.

In this image, the player has established the plane and will begin to execute the swing as he approaches the ball, based on the speed of the horse.

PLANES IN ACTION

PLANES IN ACTION

the shots

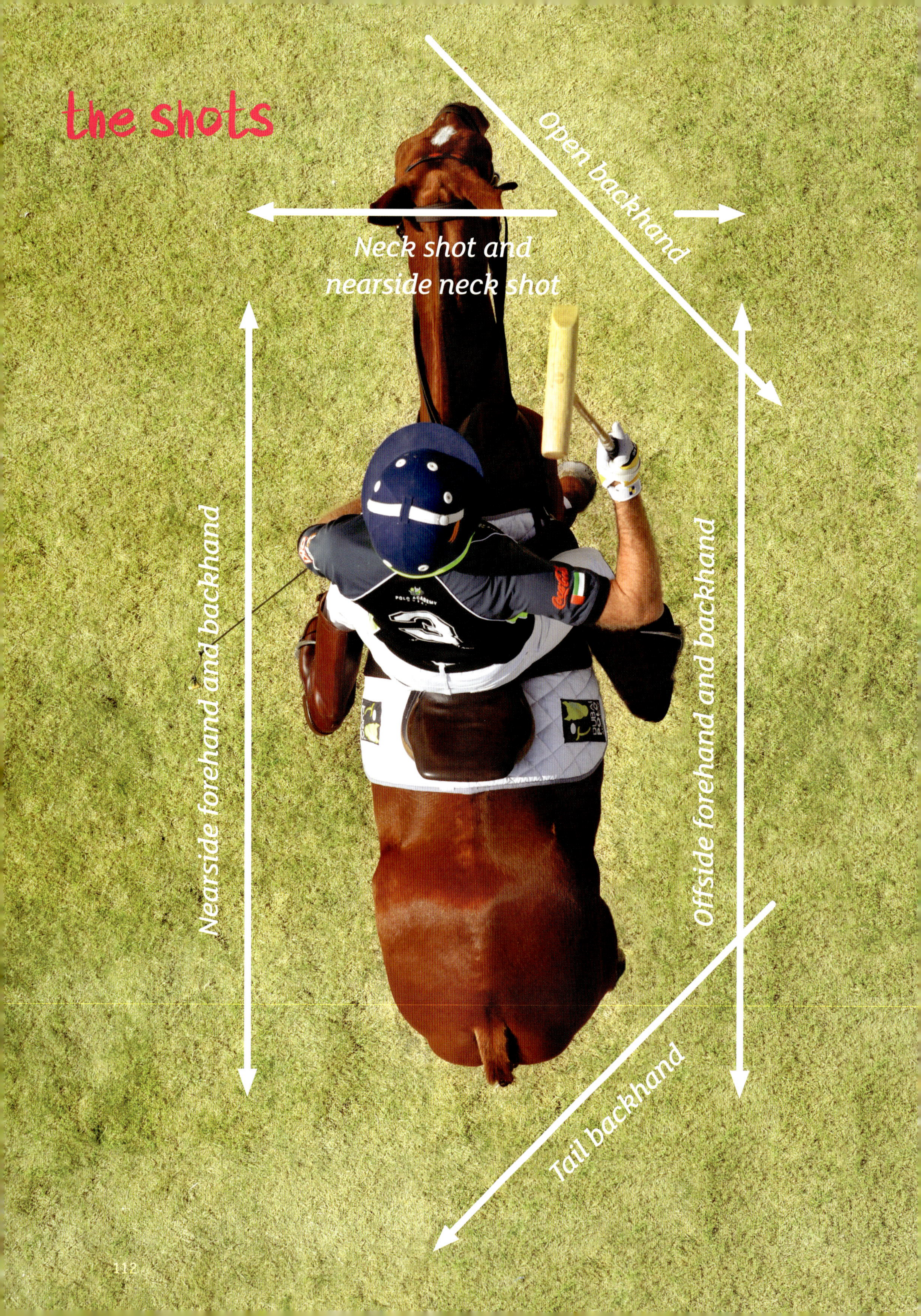

Neck shot and nearside neck shot

Open backhand

Nearside forehand and backhand

Offside forehand and backhand

Tail backhand

the ultimate top tip:
all you need is a <u>plane</u> and a <u>pendulum</u>!

04/05 THE SHOTS

HITTING THE GRID SHOTS

You will often hear that there are eight basic SHOTS around the horse. However, to be technically correct, it would be truer to say there are eight basic PLANES which you then swing through:

01 Offside forehand
02 Offside backhand
03 Nearside forehand
04 Nearside backhand
05 Open backhand
06 Tail backhand
07 Neck shot
08 Nearside neck shot

And here is the list again, but this time in the order importance of learning:

01= Offside forehand and nearside forehand
02= Open backhand and tail backhand
03= Nearside backhand and nearside neck shot
04= Neck shot and offside backhand

These are the perfect 'grid shots'. The reality is however that there is rarely a perfect environment when playing polo, so all shots will be adapted to a variation on the rules. For example, an open backhand is the term used for a shot that travels backwards at a 45 degree angle to the horse – great if the receiving player is indeed 45 degrees behind on the same plane. What though, if the player is 55, or 85 degrees behind? In that case, the hitter must find a plane that reaches him – and this statement is true for ALL hitting. So whilst we talk about the 'eight shots' around the horse, try to think more about the importance of being able to establish planes, apply a pendulum, and then use it to hit the ball.

The reality, however, is that there is only one shot: a pendulum, which is used within a structure and swung through a plane, of which there are potentially hundreds.

THE SHOTS
IN THE ORDER OF IMPORTANCE OF LEARNING *and why!*

Offside forehand

having the ability to hit on both sides will allow you to keep possession of the ball and move it forward without fouling

Nearside Forehand

Open backhand

these two ensure you have the ability to send the ball backwards but not into players behind you or whizzing past your own teammate following in support

Tail backhand

for when you have to play a defensive backhand but have arrived at the ball with it on your left

Nearside backhand

because the audience are watching and the hello magazine photographer is there!

Nearside neck shot

scoring a winning goal with this shot is guaranteed to get you some phone numbers! **boom!**

THE SHOTS CONTINUED

this is number 4 on the list because you need to train for a while to create the core strength necessary to reach for a plane way out in front of the horse's nose

Neck shot

with the open and tail backhands high up on the priority list, this is the last shot of importance because in the early stages of learning players will be following behind - so why would you hit it directly into them?

Offside backhand

TAP SHOTS

Now these little 'bad boys' are the essential shots that you need in your tool box of playing skills! There is a saying in polo: 'fastest to the ball, control on the ball'. I have witnessed many players' handicap being raised purely on their controlling skills. The inability to tap, retain and control a ball purely results in immediate panic hitting. Remember, polo is a game of whether you score more than the opposition... NOT how fast you can score – so practice keeping the ball rather than measuring success on how far you can hit it.

Possession is everything in polo. When you have the ball, you have 100 percent possession; once you have hit it, you have given away a 50 percent opportunity for the opposition to gain control. Tap shots are the smallest of all of the shots and yet they are the ones most commonly missed. The reason is generally through complacency and a weakness with the hand-to-eye coordination with the player assuming where everything is!

A tap shot in its purest form is still a pendulum. The problem is the smaller the pendulum, the smaller the characteristics it displays. The moments of suspension, acceleration and deceleration are all still there, they are just harder to identify as the momentum becomes less. This shot is just the mini version of the big 'giant pendulum' except that the wrist replaces the shoulder at the top. The hitting error occurs with beginner players when they try to 'push' the ball forward. That movement in itself forces the elbow to break and consequently raises the forearm and ultimately the stick-head over the ball.

In addition to this basic tap shot which allows you to keep the ball close, there is also another specific technique used most commonly when trying to avoid a hook. It is used when the ball is tapped as far in front of the player as he can reach. The arm is extended forward to its furthest point and uses the elasticity created in the index finger as it bends backwards pre-contact.

There is another tapping technique used when trying to avoid a hook: the ball is tapped as far in front of the player as he can reach, with the arm extended forward and use of the index finger's elasticity.

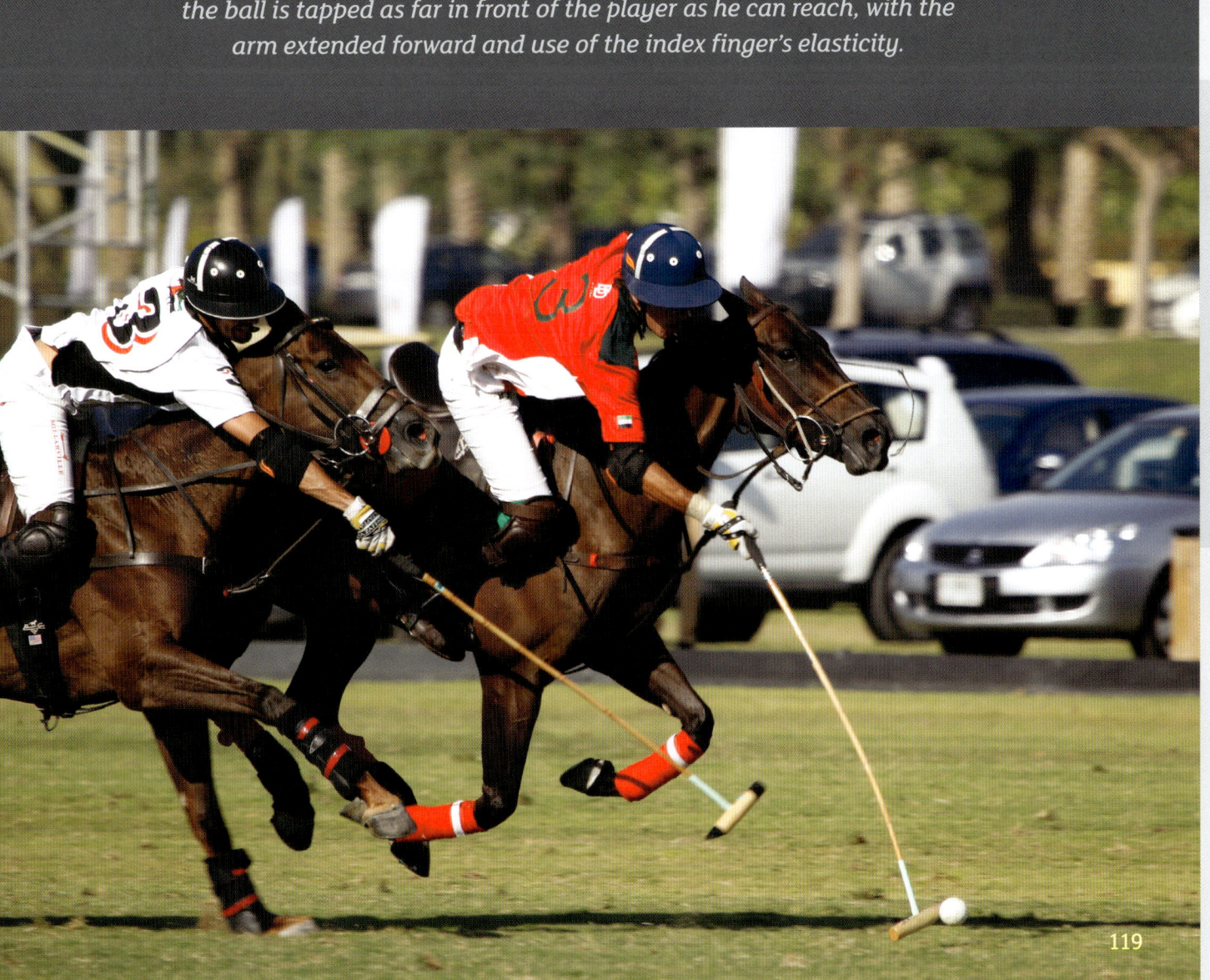

05/05 INTENTION

So with all of the shots now available to you, it's just a case of which one to use when you reach the ball. More importantly, when you do reach it, is it your intention to use a pendulum within the structure of a shot to move it, or merely make contact with it? Apparently the definition of insanity is repeating the same thing over and over and expecting a different result. Now pause for a moment and consider just how many crazy people there may be out there on the pitch!

For years I have witnessed aspiring players investing a monumental amount of time perfecting the art of imperfection. Hour after hour chasing a ball up and down, up and down desperately trying to achieve greater success. And therein lies the problem: the measure of success.

Unless there is clear intention when you swing at the ball on how far you wish it to go, and in which direction, all you will have done is vaguely moved it backwards or forwards. Unless you have a specific goal in mind, how can you know if the action itself was successful? For sure, in the early stages whilst learning, purely making contact is indeed success. However, shortly after that first glorious moment of connection, work needs to begin on consistency and skill sets to allow the player to choose distance and direction.

On the approach to the ball, a ten-goaler will instinctively know how it **feels** to be correct – therefore that is what he is aspiring to. His intention is to commit to the swing regardless of a hit or miss outcome. A beginner on the other hand will approach the ball with the intention of using any means to make contact happen between it and the mallet head.

The success of hitting lies in understanding the mechanics of how things work coupled with the disciplined art of sticking to specific techniques and resisting all instincts to 'hit at' the ball.

Take a look at the examples on the following pages and see what happens when the intention on the approach to the ball changes from producing a pendulum to hitting 'at' the object.

DEVELOPING INTENTION

The sequence below features some of my students, who can all demonstrate the start, middle, and end of an offside forehand with the intention of using a perfect pendulum to hit the ball 40 yards. However, look what happens on the approach when intention changes: the obsession under pressure is to just make contact with the ball, regardless of the distance it may travel.

1
Start

2
Middle

3
End

1

2

3

DEVELOPING INTENTION
CONTINUED

Start

Middle

End

Again, all the correct elements of the half seat, the tube, the follow through, and opposite body image are visible in the top row of images. But in the bottom row, you can see what happens when the half seat is compromised and the intention has clearly changed.

DEVELOPING INTENTION
CONTINUED

1 Start

2 Middle

3 End

1

2

3

CHAPTER CHECKLIST

You should now be able to:

 Grip the mallet correctly

 Balance the mallet vertically and be able to move it to the four main points around the horse whilst riding at any pace

 Demonstrate a perfect pendulum whilst swinging through the eight basic grid shots

 Demonstrate two types of tap shots and the body position used to achieve them

The Smiley Technique & Grid

Throughout this book, certain themes keep appearing: fluidity, fluency, elasticity. There will be nothing written about violence or aggression. These traits only lead to smacking a ball rather than creating and transferring energy to it. It should make sense that the arrival at the start of a shot has an absolute effect on what happens next. Punching or stabbing backwards creates an unbalanced jarring effect that has to be undone before the swing can begin. Equally, weak uncommitted placing of the stick on the plane will not produce the stretch required in order to continue straight and release the energy.

In this section we are going to look at a technique called a 'smiley'. The introduction of a smiley into the reach element of a shot can in an instant change the look of a player from amateur to pro as **it has an absolute effect on the rest of the body**.

The term smiley is simply the description given to the course the right hand makes as it leaves its carry position and travels to the chosen height ready for the swing. As it is in essence a curve, it collects essential component parts of the hitting machine along its journey. For the purpose of learning this technique, follow the exercise below which explains the application of the smiley technique with an offside forehand.

Exercise 12
THE SMILEY TECHNIQUE

An excellent tip to help with timing is to inhale for the smiley and exhale for the swing. The time for anyone's swing at this point should be 1.5 seconds for the smiley and the same for the swing. It is this exact timing and process that is at the very core and foundation of all hitting and should be practiced religiously until it becomes second nature.

Firstly establish a half seat position with the mallet extended out in front and on a parallel plane to the horse. (It will feel a little deliberate at this stage but we will refine it as the process develops.) Keep the shoulders and hips absolutely fixed together and allow them to move together as one.

Ensure there is no independence between right hand and left shoulder – if the right hand wrist moves back one inch the left shoulder moves forward one inch almost as if they are tied together. There should be the feeling of being quite structured and square.

Now begin the smiley by drawing a shallow curve shape in the air next to you, running parallel to the horse around shoulder height and dropping approximately five inches into its deepest part.

During the process, as the hand drops onto its downward curve, **it tips the chest forward**. As the wrist turns over, before it passes the body at the deepest part of the curve, **it draws the left shoulder over** and **engages the left groin** to make contact with the saddle – so the sequence will be to draw the mallet behind wrist, then elbow, then shoulder.

As the smiley extends to its point of stretch behind you, the shoulders will align above the horse's spine and the weight of the mallet and upper body structure will settle on the left groin.

All the essential component parts of the hitting machine are now in place, and all that remains is to find an extra two inches of stretch at the shoulder socket and swing a full pendulum to reach the exact same height opposite to where the swing began.

Remember, pendulums have characteristics, one of which is the moment of suspension. So at the end of this practice swing we can work with the gravity of the mallet, and as it drops down we can reintroduce the wrist, shoulder and pelvis rotation to repeat another smiley and continue until they all look identical. Smiley, extension, stretch, swing and suspension; and then again: smiley, extension, stretch, swing, suspension; and so on.

THE SMILEY GRID

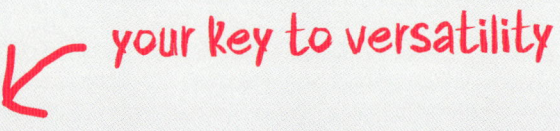 *your key to versatility*

Once you have the ability to produce a smiley, you can begin to join all of the shots together and demonstrate a 'smiley grid'. I use this training technique to help aspiring beginner players understand the importance of being able to hit on all sides of the horse from the offset. It is a swinging routine that systematically puts into place all the component parts of balance, weight transfer, momentum, and composure.

Practicing the smiley grid will build a surprising amount of subconscious muscle memory leading to a knowledge of exactly where your grid shots begin. From the carry position it is now easy to manoeuvre the stick into its relevant position – this is now a cemented hitting foundation.

The ability to complete a successful Smiley Grid is a guaranteed fast track to becoming a successful player. Initially this is quite a difficult exercise to get right but it is one of THE most important ones to master.

Remember, all that is required to hit effectively is to firstly establish a plane in the direction you wish the ball to go, then create the energy and finally expel it during a pendulum. The smiley grid, however, only requires you to work the two parallel planes running either side of the horse. The reality of the game is that rarely is there such a perfect environment, but you will now have the skill to be sufficiently versatile in the saddle to establish any one of hundreds of planes that will be necessary to expand your range of shots.

The ability to complete a successful smiley grid is a guaranteed fast track to becoming a successful player. Initially this is quite a difficult exercise to get right but it is nevertheless one of **the** most important ones to master. It is made up of a series of swings around the horse all joined together with smileys and all displaying pendulum characteristics.

do the balance and technique exercise on the next page to complete a smiley grid!

The purpose of the smiley grid is to highlight if and where any balance points are 'off' and secondly, it reinforces the essential technique of 'body hitting and over-arm hitting'. It also challenges the ability to be versatile when coupled with the horse's movement, especially at speed.

It is an all-too-common sight in low goal polo matches around the world to see players racing down the pitch trying get distance on the ball. However, they are only able to achieve a nine o'clock position with their arm extended behind due to the restriction of the pelvis and subsequent inability to drive their left shoulder towards their right groin.

> As demonstrated above, the all-too-common problem of players with a fixed pelvis rather than a versatile one that can move together with the shoulders results in the inability to reach for the power shots behind. Instinctively, if players do not feel they have created energy and elasticity they will simply attempt to hit AT the ball rather than swinging a complete pendulum with the body.

really really important!

Exercise 13
THE SMILEY GRID

This exercise is best performed using the back line of the pitch as a guide. This allows you to judge how balanced your riding position is during the hitting process whilst testing your versatility

Start at point A on the plane, with the chest square and facing forwards

Swing a perfect pendulum **BACKWARDS** to arrive at point B, until the left groin touches the saddle

Aim to stack the left shoulder directly below the right wrist. Finally, swing a giant pendulum until the body position mirrors that of image 3 above

Continue drawing back until you reach your offside plane and stretch as high as you can. Left groin touches the saddle and chest faces right

in the saddle. Ensure that you begin with a pure pendulum containing the characteristics of acceleration, deceleration, and moment of suspension to set the benchmark for every swing. Once you are able to produce the routine at a stand, take it up a level and perform it at canter. The measure of success will be whether you are able to reach the ground with the mallet with each stroke on both sides of the horse without leaning or without him faultering off his course.

Swing a complete pendulum forward until the right groin touches the saddle and the chest is facing left

Drop a smiley across the body until the forearm reaches a parallel plane on the nearside with the mallet as far **BEHIND** you as possible

Drop a **DEEP** smiley, almost to belt height, ensuring pelvis and shoulders are fixed together as they rotate to allow chest to face right by sinking slightly left

Swing a pure pendulum to a position just slightly higher than your head in front on the nearside

THE NEARSIDE IN ISOLATION

To look at the nearside as a separate subject is really rather contradictory to my methodology, however as the nearside creates such misery, frustration, and disappointment to a new player's life, I thought it would be appropriate to give it its own little section as a testament to its ability to thoroughly ruin someone's day!

Now the rules of polo clearly state 'the player who is entitled to hit the ball is the first player to establish the line'. And what if the line is established by approaching it from the right? The only available shot to use is on the nearside.

Fouling by crossing the line to go for your favourite offside shot is not an option, so there should be equal importance as a beginner to develop nearside shots as much as offside ones. Over twenty years of teaching, I've always been surprised by the number of novice players who consider the nearside 'the dark side of town' when actually, once a correct offside shot is achievable, nearside positioning already exists. The pelvic and leg position on completion of an offside

END of OFFSIDE forehand

START of NEARSIDE backhand

same same!

The pelvic and leg position on completion of an offside forehand is the same as at the beginning of a nearside backhand, which is also the same as the finish of a nearside forehand

forehand is exactly the same at the beginning of a nearside backhand, i.e., right groin touching the saddle and chest facing left. This reinforces the importance of versatility in the saddle as **without the ability to rotate the pelvis, there will always be restriction on the number of planes you can find, especially on the nearside.**

really important

> **Over twenty years of teaching, I've always been surprised by the number of novice players who consider the nearside 'the dark side of town' when actually, once a correct offside shot is achievable, nearside positioning already exists.**

I wonder sometimes that if in a player's very first polo lesson the emphasis was on the nearside forehand as the most important shot, would the offside then become the 'scary side' when it is attempted several weeks down the line?

The trick to developing successful nearside forehand shots in the early stages of learning is to accept two basic principles: The direction a ball will travel when hit on the near side is 100 percent dependent on which way the elbow was pointing and which plane the forearm had adopted. If you watch beginners playing or an inexperienced student attempt a nearside forehand, it is predictable way before contact that the ball will more often than not go under the horse's neck to the right.

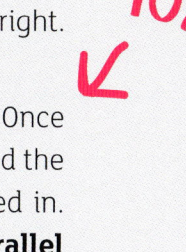
see pg 107

The reason for this: remember the two sheets of glass analogy? Once the forearm is placed in the plane, it must complete its course and the mallet head will finish exactly opposite to the position it started in. The only way to get a ball to travel forward in a straight line **parallel** to the horse is if the position of the arm is established and is kept in a parallel plane to the horse until the shot is completed.

In summary, the secret to success of all hitting is about having the confidence in the mechanics and physics of how things work. **Remember, we never hit at the object. Instead we have an intention to establish a plane, and swing a complete pendulum – the ball just happens to be in the way!**

time to train the brain!

~~The Hitting Process~~

THE CHECKLIST

If I was asked to program a computerised robot to hit a polo ball with an offside forehand, take a look at the list on the next page of required basic necessities! The reason I have gone into extreme detail with this list is to help with motivation when first learning to hit the ball, and by that I mean hitting it cleanly and properly. There are an astonishing number of things that you need to get right in order to do just that.

The overriding message here: accept that it is not initially that difficult to hit 'at' the ball and move it forward. The trick is to create a 'machine' that will open up a whole new world of hitting opportunities by hitting it well and technically correctly. The more you practice, the more parts you get right and then bank into muscle memory. Remember you are new to this, so you are allowed to go through the learning curve and can afford to be nice to yourself rather than frustrated! And think on: you are **training**, so in the early stages it is much more beneficial to complete a training session having banked more good muscle memory than bad, regardless of how many times you hit the ball.

THE ONE AND ONLY OFFICIAL HITTING PROCESS CHECKLIST

(offside forehand)

01 Start with the mallet in a vertical position

02 Balance the weight on the base of the index finger

03 Roll into a half seat

04 Sink down onto the knees

05 Open the toes

06 Push away with the inside ball of the feet

07 Push the heels down

08 Bend the wrist back on itself and establish a plane by drawing the elbow backwards

09 Keep the mallet vertical at all times

10 Allow the left shoulder to follow the motion

11 Support the body weight on the left groin

12 Reach to your chosen height behind you by pushing your left shoulder towards your right groin

13 Support the mallet on the base of the index finger

14 Find an extra stretch at the right shoulder socket

15 Allow the chin to come to rest on the chest

16 Ensure the mallet is at right angles with the forearm

17 Fix the pelvis and shoulders together

18 Start the swing sequence by lifting the left shoulder high and back

19 Allow gravity to pull the mallet down in a vertical motion

20 Use the left shoulder as the driving mechanism for the swing

21 Ensure the right shoulder socket is stretched at all times

22 Sweep the mallet along the floor

23 Complete a full pendulum

24 Wait until the shoulder "tells" the chin to look up

25 Finish by looking straight down the hitting arm

now memorise it!

here's something else that will help...

PERCEPTION AND HEIGHT DEFICITS: HIT BY PRODUCING THE "D" SHAPE

In the early stages of learning to hit the ball, especially if relatively new to riding, it is quite comforting to remain in the saddle and right at the last minute lean out and 'swipe' in an effort to make contact. We already know that this hit-at motion will rarely get the required results and it is potentially dangerous for both rider and horse. It is important therefore to accept that the length of the polo mallet was designed to be used with a good half seat together with a specific technique in order to reach the ground – if you remain seated the mallet is actually too short to reach the ground without leaning.

The trick to swinging fluidly and remaining balanced is to actually use the LEFT shoulder to begin the swinging process. As it is rolled high and back, the shoulder automatically redresses the original height deficit whilst keeping the body balanced. It feels like an arching away from the ball as the swing is executed and it allows for weight over the horse to remain consistent. At the point of contact it should feel like you are trying to create a 'D' shape with the body.

top tip

Rolling the left shoulder high and back ensures a body hit and cleanly sends the energy down the shaft

MAKING CONTACT

Throughout this book, I have tried to go into as much detail as possible about positioning and techniques to allow any aspiring player to actually feel how it feels to be correct. Unlike tennis or golf where an instructor can stand behind a beginner and physically manoeuvre them into the correct stance, polo has to be learned by vision or explanation. By now you are well aware that there is a sequence of events that must take place in order to hit a ball. The ball itself is only three inches in diameter so

Exercise 14
WORKING BACKWARDS

Firstly, establish a deep balanced half seat on a still horse allowing the mallet to hang directly to the floor. Open up the chest and pull the shoulder blades back together until almost touching. Begin to bend the right lower leg allowing the knee to sink slightly, twisting the chest to face slightly left in the process (yes this is not a typo – chest LEFT!). Focus now on getting the right groin hard into the saddle and lifting the left shoulder as high as possible and pull it behind. This motion will start to create an arch on the right side of the body – the more this position is stretched to its furthest points, the lower the mallet will get to the ground. The legs should still be close to the horse with a significant push down through the right heel, and the right knee squeezing closed against the saddle which will intensify the elastic feeling in the left lower back.

Start with the mallet hanging directly below the shoulder...

Turn the palm of the hand to face out and use the right arm to draw the mallet up to a vertical position...

margin for error is huge. Now whilst you can strive to produce a perfect hitting machine under the pressures of a match, the reality is that things will be hurried or missed out – the machine will still function but just not as efficiently and there are really only two outcomes: either you're going to hit the ball or you're going to miss it! Therefore, for the best possible chance of success, you need to look at the exact point of contact and the various stages that bring you to the moment of impact. Always remember that the stick is applied to a bodily motion and it only truly stretches to the ground when it is physically swung.

It is the release of this stored power that will ultimately move the ball. With the chest now to the left, the shoulders will almost be stacked and in line parallel above the horse's spine. Finally, using the muscles at the back of the neck, bend the neck until the chin touches the chest. This allows the chin to rest against the shoulder and look straight down the stick. The mallet at this point should still not be touching the ground because the final redress is the stretch at the shoulder socket which is produced when it begins to swing. At this point everything should still feel completely balanced, pulling away to the left and centring the weight above the horse with the left shoulder as the extreme highest point, then head, hand and finally mallet head. From here, work backwards through the shot as that will present greater mechanical characteristics and sensations of how it actually feels to be correct. The other advantage of doing it this way is that it will allow the manufacture of the exact route the mallet would have and should have taken from its start position. Additionally, it allows identification of where, when and which parts of the body need to move to accommodate the weight shift as the body rotates. Finally it will also allow you to find exactly where the power packs are located.

When the arm is at a nine o'clock position, consciously fix the body frame and push the left shoulder to the right groin...

This automatically lifts the right arm and you'll feel the energy being created in the lower back

back to the physics!

> Apply Newton's Third Law: For every action there is an equal and opposite reaction. And so, using the technique of rolling the left shoulder high and back will send the energy in the opposite direction down the shaft of the mallet.

HITTING DISCIPLINE

It goes without saying that there is an awful lot of pressure when playing polo, and a multitude of things to concentrate on. It is hardly surprising that beginners often miss the ball when playing in a game or match, despite their success and consistency when out stick and balling. I recall vividly when I had just begun polo being totally overwhelmed by the pressure of my own performance, an audience, team expectations and the possibility of making embarrassing fouls. Hardly a relaxed frame of mind to then approach and hit the ball calmly and fluidly! However, the trick I learned to help me overcome and blinker myself from all of the distractions was **to focus on a systematic checklist that I had rehearsed during every stick and ball session:** I knew what my perfect half seat felt like and so in a game on the approach to a ball it was number one on the list to sink

lower until I found it. I knew I wanted to hit the ball 60 yards, for example, so I inhaled for 1.5 seconds as I reached for the ten o'clock position behind me. At that point I found an extra two inches of stretch from within my shoulder socket. I also simulated the mallet had a five kilogram weight strapped to the stick head and focussed on letting my shoulder stretch through the revolution of the swing. When the shot began, I exhaled and calmly counted in my mind another 1.5 seconds to complete the swing.

"breathe, pendulum, swing slowly!"

"hit it, kill it, destroy it!"

Finally, I pictured what I looked like from the side and if the audience had to use three words to describe what they had just seen they would be elastic, fluid, and graceful.

Creating a personal checklist and recounting it on the way to the ball can really help as a distraction from all the external pressures. The trick is to practice, practice, practice so as to know exactly how it feels to be correct at different points and by so doing, know the feelings you are aspiring to feel as you approach and execute your swing under pressure. Never listen to the little hitting devil who is guaranteed to appear on your shoulder, whispering some BIG FAT LIES!

ACCURACY ON DISTANCE

The simple principle of hitting is that the further away from the ball you take the mallet head, the more elasticity, energy, power, and momentum you can build up. Having the ability to hit far is great – if the player you are passing to is halfway down the pitch. But what if he is only 30 yards away? Good players instinctively know where to begin their shot so the ball lands in the most convenient place possible for their team mate to make the next play. It is a great skill to be able to hit a huge ball over the top of your own players' heads, but remember, once you have released it there is only a 50/50 chance that *your* player will win the horse race to get to it ahead of the opposition. Think of it like a basketball game: the player with the ball keeps it until he **passes it accurately** to his team mate; he doesn't throw it wildly in the air, vaguely in the direction of scoring in the hope that one of his own team mates will get to it first!

see pg 179

Exercise 15
THE CLOCK

Firstly, you need a horse that is calm and consistent in canter. Ideally, also an assistant and the use of a pitch to allow you to measure results. As this exercise is about banking the muscle memory for arm positioning, you are going to use a training technique called 'The Clock'. It is effectively an imaginary clock face next to you on the right with number twelve above your head and number six on the ground. Adopt a half seat on the stationary horse and point the right arm directly behind to a nine o'clock position; then swing a pure pendulum through to settle at three o'clock. Repeat this for a ten, eleven, and midnight position, each time ensuring that the pendulum is true and pure with all of its characteristics clearly visible. Once confident of the location of each position, have the assistant space some balls equally on the back line of the pitch.

To get a fair average on how far your nine, ten, eleven, and twelve o'clock shots reach, you ideally need to hit ten balls at each position. Begin by establishing a healthy consistent canter and circle around ensuring on the approach to each ball there is a minimum of five straight strides. There is no target in this exercise so **the measure of success should be based on the quality of the swing and not on the distance the balls reach.**

To help with consistency, start the swing at the same point each time in front at shoulder level and swing a reverse pendulum to its required position. Regardless of its starting height, the pendulum swing count is 'one and...' for 1.5 seconds. The majority of players at all levels that have completed this exercise are astonished at how much unnecessary effort they have been applying to achieve distance when the reality is that all the power was already there. The trick now is to repeat the exercise, reaching all of the clock positions, but starting from the normal 'carry position', and apply a smiley. It is essential that discipline remains intact throughout so as not to disrupt the integrity of the pendulum as you build the structure around the shot and produce elasticity with the body.

As you play and become stronger and more proficient, this exercise should be used frequently **to monitor and gauge hitting performance. It will clearly highlight which areas have swapped technique for strength.**

You should aspire to feel the same stretch at the shoulder as you would hanging vertically with the right arm from a bar. Only when this is achieved is there a clear channel for the energy and consistency with the shoulder rotation.

POWER HITTING, PENALTIES AND PRE-SWINGS

Without the feeling that you have indeed created elastic to hit the ball, you will instinctively and incorrectly try to hit the ball harder and faster - the consequence of which is the destruction of the 'hitting machine'. The ball is likely to be topped as the body snatches at it, the shoulders lift as they brace for impact, and all of the power is absorbed as you fall back in the saddle due to the speed of the stick.

If you've got this far in the book, you should now have all the key fundamentals in place for the half seat, the grip, the plane, and a pendulum, and you can now look at turning this efficient bodily machine of balance and versatility into an energy creator. The power in a shot is largely generated by the amount of elastic that you can produce within the natural restraints of the mechanics of the body.

The feeling just before releasing a 'power shot' is the same as pulling an enormous bow and arrow – the bow is drawn back to an extreme point, the energy is stored and then released. Remember in the earlier section we talked about full rotation of the shoulder socket and how the feeling of ultimate stretching becomes more apparent. When

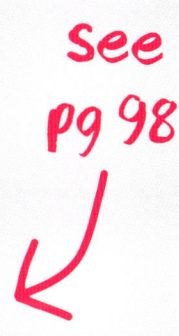

See pg 98

> **The power in a shot is largely generated by the amount of elastic that you can produce within the natural restraints of the mechanics of the body.**

placing the stick at any point on the clock you should aspire to feel the same stretch at the shoulder as you would hanging vertically with the right arm from a bar. Only when this is achieved is there a clear channel for the energy and consistency with the shoulder rotation.

This technique also allows you to simulate the mallet head being much heavier than it actually is, allowing you to build up much more momentum and club head speed. Isolating the shoulder in this manner will also aid in swinging at the right speed rather than snatching at the ball by pulling the stick with hand and forearm.

push and lift!
Fixing the right wrist and left shoulder together

With shoulders fixed, the right wrist will lift to an exact point opposite

push the left shoulder down to the right groin.

All of your hard work to date will pay off as you should now have enough balance and core stability to create a power shot. The original smiley stabiliser that produced the essential pelvic versatility can now be dispensed with and replaced with a sophisticated straight arm and body pulling action.

The upcoming exercise outlines how to produce a pre-swing. The benefit of adding a pre-swing to the shot automatically reminds you of the essential parts and mechanics that you will ultimately be using as part of your main shot.

POWER HITTING

Back to the physics!

more physics, huh...

All correct swinging from any point to its opposite point takes 1.5 seconds. Watching polo might convince you that players hit the ball much quicker than this. Yes, sometimes they do when the environment is not perfect and they are under pressure to avoid being hooked for example, but remember you are aspiring to 'perfect hitting', from which you will learn to adapt.

When training you constantly have to reinforce a perfect 'home position and technique' so that it is the only thing in the subconscious when you go to hit with an instinctive reflex reaction - it's from here that all other hitting techniques and variations will evolve.

Here are the five areas of power creation:

01 The lower back: the more you twist and distort the upper body, the more intensity you feel in the lower back. **When you think you've managed to twist to the max, twist five inches more!**

02 A total rotation of the pelvis. The more you are able to rotate the pelvis, the more you will create an opportunity to take the stick and arm higher behind and above the head.

03 When the mallet motion is reversed: a mallet travelling in one direction and then pulled in the opposite direction before the moment of suspension is truly complete. Generally seen in pure pendulum swings that reach eleven o'clock or midnight.

04 The elastic created between the index finger and stick, and its release when the angle explodes to a straight position at contact.

05 When the shoulder blades are pulled back together and almost touch, significant amount of stretch across the chest is produced.

Exercise 16
THE PRE-SWING

1 Begin with the mallet in the normal 'carry' position

2 Draw the mallet backwards along the parallel plane to the horse, dropping down to an area level with the horse's back

3

4

Lock the elbow and, using the right shoulder, swing the forearm forwards. Allow the momentum to pull the body into a half seat and allow the forearm to decelerate to a point around five o'clock. There will be gathering momentum in the mallet which will continue to travel when the forearm is restricted. Allow the mallet to climb until it reaches a 90 degree angle between it and the forearm.

5

6

Drive the left shoulder towards the right groin and draw the mallet in a straight line to an 11 o'clock position above the head. Complete a full, powerful pendulum. Whether you aspire to use a pre-swing or adopt a style allowing you to raise the mallet above the head, from its normal carry position, you MUST in both cases accurately travel along the 5/11 line without faltering. Ask someone to film you at a standstill and see how easy it is to drop off a 5/11 course without driving the left shoulder technique.

Follow the journey of the hand and see how accurate and deliberate the structure is.

THE PRE-SWING CRIME SCENE *Call the polo police!*

The general mistake in a pre-swing is when the swing itself lacks control and gathers too much momentum. As a result it can often finish as high as four o'clock. The consequence is the arm ends up creating a windmill effect as it drawn to the back of the shot or is dragged in a straight line only to reach its opposite point. In this example, the 'draw' started at three-thirty and arrived at nine-thirty on the clock. No power or elasticity was generated.

Compare both shapes above!

now see it in action!

3

Look how defined and symmetrical this player's pre-swing and shot is compared to the weak example on the previous page.

6

remember...
the journey is more important than the destination!

INDIVIDUAL STYLE
everyone is different!

Everyone is an individual and made up differently, and it is why no two players look the same when compared like-for-like under identical circumstances. It is also the reason why you should be careful when watching other players and trying to adopt their technique as it works specifically for them, and them only. Everyone looks different. Style evolves from this very fact but as always, everyone's hitting will visibly have all of the fundamentals in place.

Here's an example of several pros executing neck shots. Whilst all of the golden rules of hitting are in place, they all look distinctly different. Player style is down to bodily make-up. So whilst it is hugely beneficial to watch pros in action, make sure you follow the rules and allow your own personal style to evolve.

PITCH-SIDE TRAINING

Practicing with hand sticks in the early stages of learning can help enormously to understand how the mallet works and how you need to accommodate the swing with a **bodily movement.** However, be aware that anyone walking normally has a natural swing with their arms across their body – and not a parallel swinging action like marching. Equally, the action of walking means one leg is always behind the other. The consequence is that walking up to and hitting a ball with a hand mallet does not actually simulate hitting a polo ball on a horse very much at all.

Having spent many hours dismantling players' swinging problems who had developed an across-the-body swing, I took it upon myself to produce an alternative training aid.

When walking, one leg is always behind the other - unlike the position you ultimately need to adopt on a horse where the thighs are together.

In addition, most swings finish up like tennis shots, i.e., across the chest, which ultimately means the mallet would hit the horse in the head.

This really simple but revolutionary aid is called the **PitchJunkie Core Trainer**™. It is designed to highlight any hitting and balance problems immediately. These training mats have four planes drawn on them for guidance which allow a player to see where the imperfections in the swing are located. More importantly, each mat is fitted with a pressure sensor under the feet which sounds an alarm each time a player leans.

Only when a player's core strength is developed sufficiently will he or she be able to complete a clearly defined swinging regime without sounding the alarm. If you don't have access to one of these training mats, you can still complete your own self-analysis using the following exercise:

- Take a hand-stick together with two books or similar and partially stand on them allowing the simulation of the feet being positioned in the stirrups with the heels down.

- Now place the mallet at various hitting points behind the body to simulate the start of an offside forehand.

- As the mallet gains height the pressure onto the right foot will increase.

- At this stage, equalise the balance by bending the left knee and accommodating the twist in the pelvis.

- The higher the stick climbs the greater the requirement to compensate on to the left groin – a couple of minutes spent completing a smiley grid will certainly allow you to identify the real core muscles you should have been using to support your shots.

With the aid of pressure sensors under the feet, a player can identify the exact point where any imbalance begins...

And with the aid of ground lines to simulate planes, an instructor can identify exactly where the swing needs adjustment...

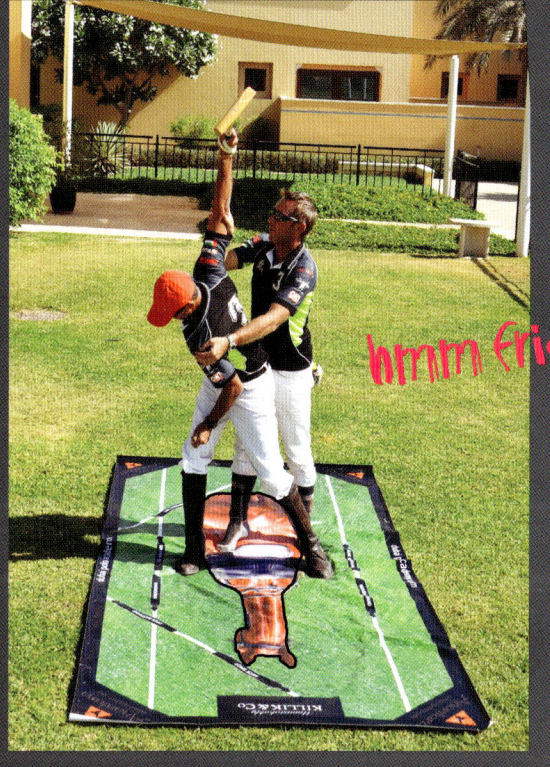

hmm friendly!

Without the added distraction of a horse, these mats have drastically improved many players' techniques. The alarm sensors under the feet expose excessive leaning whilst the inability to reach all planes around the horse highlights areas of riding weakness leading to lack of versatility in the saddle.

order your pro-trainer mat online at pitchjunkie.ae!

CHAPTER CHECKLIST

You should now be able to:

 Demonstrate a 'smiley'

 Swing through a 'smiley grid' at all paces, reaching the ground on both sides

 Produce a 'D' shape consistently on contact when executing an offside forehand

 Recall and recite your personal hitting checklist

 Identify your individual body power packs

 Hit a variety of shots to various distances consistently

 Produce a pre-swing

 Demonstrate a pre-swing and a power shot together

PART III:
~~APPLICATION~~
scoring on and off the field

Stick ~~and Balling~~ it all together and Hitting Diagnostics

As obvious as it sounds, stick and balling is all about **practicing the skills needed to play the game**. In addition, just as a horse will be schooled several times in between matches, a player also needs to keep resetting perfect techniques which are very often compromised during the chaos of a game. Ideally a stick and ball session should be approached with the same mentality as going to the gym for a workout. For example, you wouldn't go to a gym, do three mediocre sit-ups and then run to the mirror to admire your new six-pack! So be as disciplined about training as an athlete would be in any other sport.

Constant repetition of the correct technique over time will get the required results whilst allowing the build-up of essential muscle memory. It is paramount to have a plan for each session. A properly devised plan will maintain focus, motivation, and discipline whilst allowing measurement of success.

If you have reached this far in the book and are able to demonstrate all of the exercises successfully, you are well on your way to becoming a very efficient and effective player. If however, you are not getting the results you set out to achieve then it is time for a polo medical check-up! You should be a well-oiled hitting machine. So if something is going wrong, just keep reminding yourself that 'it's not that you can't do it - it's just that you are not doing it right.' Put more simply, a part of the machine is broken so you need to find out what it is and why it's bust.

If your car isn't running smoothly or starts to make a strange noise, it would make sense that you take it to a diagnostics centre to locate the problem – so in this instance you are going to do the equivalent and put all your skills under the microscope for an examination. Remember, polo is just physics: you need versatility to find planes, and once you find them, you stick in a pendulum – the ball 'just happens' to be in the way. To increase the range and distance of the shots is a matter of suppleness, which allows you to create elasticity in the body, and stability, to maintain the riding position.

Exercise 17
STICK AND BALL

The following stick and ball exercise is designed to look at the purity of the skill sets. It combines a test of balance, fluidity, versatility, elasticity, control, pure pendulums, and mental discipline.

Step 1: At the side of the pitch, complete ten smiley grids whilst standing still.

Step 2: Get warmed up with five minutes combination of sitting and rising trot in figure of eights.

Step 3: Canter in a straight line for the full length of pitch, performing ten smiley grids with no ball, ensuring the mallet head sweeps the grass on both sides.

Step 4: Maintain healthy canter rhythm and circle around and re-enter the pitch, collect a ball and begin with pure pendulums working ONLY ten to two o'clock. Do not measure success on how far the ball travels. Instead, focus on inhaling for the back-swing over 1.5 seconds, exhaling for the pendulum over 1.5 seconds, and ensure the body position is a complete mirror image either side of contact. **Complete 50 reps.**

Step 5: Introduce a smiley to the swing and find a two-inch stretch at the shoulder socket and swing a classic offside forehand on completion of the shot, smiley again and repeat the exercise. Focus on the shoulder socket stretch and the quality of the pendulum during the swing. **Complete 50 reps. Don't measure success on distance the ball travels but on the quality of the swing.**

Step 6: Repeat the above exercise and, assuming the shot was finished correctly with the right groin in and chest facing left, **introduce each time** a smiley across the body to the near side. **The forearm must have met a parallel plane to the horse with the elbow pointing forwards.**

Complete a pendulum swing to achieve a nearside forehand and finish at two o'clock. At the moment of suspension, fix the shoulders and pelvis together and use the whole of the body to draw the stick through another deep smiley down to waist level and then straight up as high as you can get, ideally to eleven o'clock, and then swing a final offside forehand. Ensure that, upon completion at one o'clock, the body is a mirror image of how it began i.e., chest now to the left, with right groin touching the saddle.

Bring the stick back to the carry position and maintain a half seat and continue to the next ball. Be very clear that in this phase of the exercise you should only be hitting the ball with an offside forehand and sending it approximately 40 to 60 yards ahead of you. This will give you the time to complete all of the other swings in succession with the emphasis on rhythm, tempo, balance, versatility, and the purity of the pendulums within the swings.

Step 7: Tapping: The trick to completing this exercise is to practice and be aware how powerful your tap shot can be unintentionally. So the goal is to keep the ball one to one and a half metres ahead of you to allow a tap every one to three seconds.

Exercise 17
CONTINUED

It is essential in the early stages to learn to tap on both sides of the horse to ensure equal development. Stay loose at the wrist and flexible and elastic at the base of the right index finger. If you miss the ball, keep your rhythm and tempo and circle back to a point where you have a clean approach. **Never stop and partially turn back. Maintain composure.**

Between the tap shots constantly look up and around as this is ultimately what will happen during the reality of a game. On completion of three circles of tapping make your way back up the field to the back-line using giant pendulums, eleven o'clock to one o'clock. **Now stop and take a breather!**

Step 9: 'Sink Left, Sink Right': Revisit the exercise and complete ten *sink left, sink right* whilst standing still, ensuring your **shoulders are stacking above the horse's spine**. On completion of the tenth *sink right*, the chest is now absolutely facing left. Place the forearm on a 45-degree plane, look over the right shoulder down to the ground and execute an open backhand swing. Resume a carry position, square half seat, and sink to the left. Stack the shoulders above the horse's spine, chest to the right, and place the forearm on a 45-degree plane, look down, and execute a tail shot. On completion of ten practice swings, canter back onto the pitch. Have a ball placed on the 30-yard line and approach it square on.

Step 10: Zigzag Backhand Track: On arrival at the ball, complete an open backhand and hit the ball to arrive on or near the backline, circle around to the right and on arrival at the ball hit a tail shot so the ball reaches on or near to the 30-yard line, circle round again and continue the sequence of open backhands and tail backhands using the backline and 30-yard line as guides.

The benefit of using a 30-yard distance is that it creates lightness in the saddle and no power is used to send the ball. Coupled with a calm rhythm and tempo from the horse, the actions begin to flow rather than develop into a violent and wild 'hammer' hitting style. **Remember, energy conservation is what we are after.**

Whilst initially this exercise may appear complicated, I devised it to ensure that the emphasis was on the versatility required in the saddle to achieve the two parallel planes running next to the horse. Because half of the exercise is actually without a ball, more emphasis can be placed on the quality of the swing and the importance of being able to establish planes, both of which are only possible when the left and right groin technique is used.

The tapping element really focusses and trains essential hand-to-eye coordination. The backhand phase is based on the principle that if you are able to produce a perfect pendulum on the offside – beginning with chest to the right, left groin touching, and finishing chest to the left, right groin touching, you already have the body position to perform an open backhand and a tail backhand.

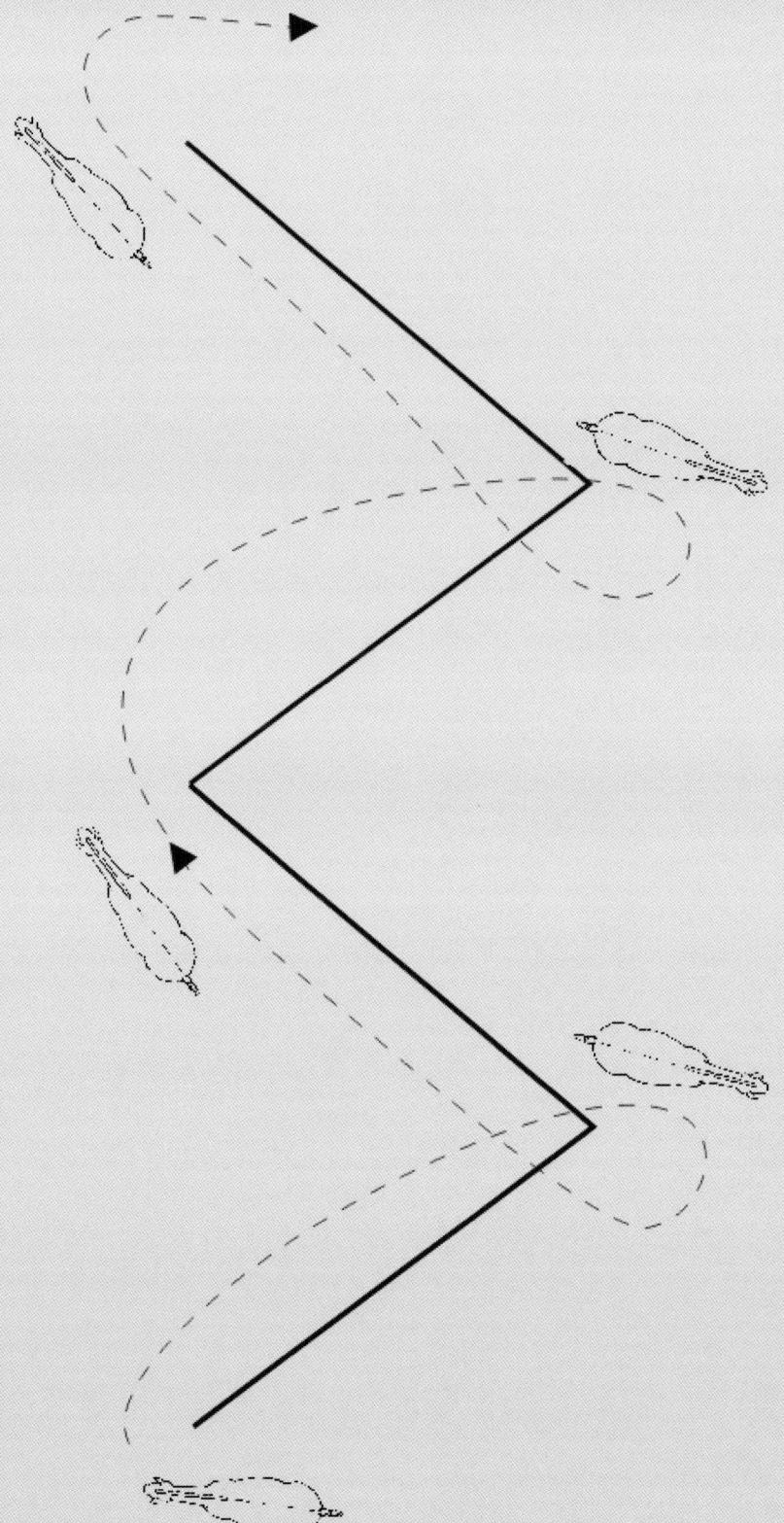

You can end the exercise with a freestyle session incorporating the more difficult advanced shots as your balance and stability allows, i.e.:

- neck shot
- nearside neck shot
- nearside backhand
- nearside tail shot
- open nearside backhand
- straight backhand

The reason I specifically left these out of the exercise is that to achieve them safely and successfully, a player needs to have significant core strength. You should really try to introduce one or two of the above shots every time you practice.

You may also notice that I have left out both the offside straight backhand and the nearside straight backhand, the reason being that they are just the offside forehand and nearside forehand in reverse, and therefore technically speaking they are already achievable. However, I do have an enormous aversion to teaching straight backhands based on the fact that during a game there are usually players following in your tracks directly behind, therefore why hit a ball directly backwards into them, or send it whizzing past your own supporting player!

173

I often encourage my students to **use the analogy of a gymnast performing a specific move and then being awarded marks out of ten for its technical merit, and in this case, all of the characteristics that make up a perfect swing (moment of suspension, creation of elastic, acceleration phase, deceleration phase, another moment of suspension).** The benefit of doing this is that it calls for focus on the swing itself, and leads to a banking of good muscle memory, the key to success when looking for instant reactions in the game. This 'perfect way' is all that you will have left in the subconscious.

TEAM CHAT

Developing overall hitting ability is rather like building a house. You need to layer the whole structure and be really disciplined about waiting to build the next storey to the house only when the previous one is solid and sound.

It is extremely tempting to just go out and hit a ball around and then see how far it will go, but a couple of weeks in the early stages perfecting the art of perfection, and then building upon it will ensure that you end up loving polo rather than being constantly frustrated by it.

Discipline, dedication, and constant practice will bring success on the field.

There is a great story, which could be urban myth, but I will share it with you all the same! After winning the Gold Cup at Cowdray Park, it will come as no surprise that there were mass celebrations and all the players of the winning team took the following day off. All but one that is – Adolfo Cambiaso. The man named as the greatest player in the world, having retained his ten-goal handicap since the age of 19, could be seen the day after the finals, stick and balling. When questioned why he wasn't resting after winning one of the sport's most prestigious tournaments, he replied, 'I missed a backhand yesterday...!' If ever there was an example of discipline, dedication, and practice makes perfect, I guess this is it.

graduation!

Playing

WHEN IT FINALLY COMES TO THAT GLORIOUS GRADUATION DAY WHEN ALL THE HARD WORK AND EFFORT CAN BE REALIZED AND THE FIRST INSTRUCTIONAL CHUKKA IS ABOUT TO BEGIN, THE TASK IS NOW MORE MENTAL THAN PHYSICAL.

Not wanting to state the obvious again, but polo is a team game, therefore every play made or not made (as the case may be) **must** be for the benefit of the team. For this reason, I have chosen not to write endless pages on the rules of polo because team captains and coaches at the club where you play are well able to explain them all in detail. Plus, it is much easier to understand with live demonstrations! Instead, what I want to get across in this chapter is the mindset with which you should enter a game.

Polo is not a game of 'how fast you can score', but more one of simply scoring more goals than the opposition. You certainly won't be able to do it single handedly, and successful teams are those with team members who trust and rely on their team mates for support and also protection.

Polo is not a game of 'how fast you can score', but more one of simply scoring more goals than the opposition. You certainly won't be able to do it single handedly, and **successful teams are those with team members who trust and rely on their team mates for support and also protection.**

To reinforce this message of team solidarity and trust, and to put it in absolute context, imagine being two metres from the goal, with the ball, and about to score in the last five seconds of the Polo World Cup in front of an audience of 20,000 spectators. A team mate behind shouts 'leave it'! Wow – it is going to take some painful discipline to do just that! However, never forget, the team mate who shouted it has the same intention – to win. With your head down, focussing on the ball, you can't see what he can see, and he would probably have a completely justified reason for shouting: perhaps you are about to foul, the consequence of which would be play stopped and reversed; perhaps an opponent is about to violently hook and disturb the perfectly placed ball for him to hit. It could be any number of reasons, but it comes down to the fact that he is likely to be shouting for all the right ones and not just to take the glory of scoring the winning goal for himself (one would hope and pray!) The point is: all team members must be aware of everyone's skill sets and there must be trust amongst each other. So, if it's your first game or chukka, you need to try to accept that for much of the time your job is not to chase the ball but to protect the player who has the ball.

> **You need to try to accept that for much of the time your job is not to chase the ball but to protect the player who has the ball.**

If he has support, he can continue making positive plays. But more importantly, if he does miss the ball, his back is covered and you are on hand to pick it up. There is no question that it will be tempting when you first get out there to fall into the trap that the ball is there to be hit and you are going to fly like the wind down the pitch and score! Whilst the enthusiasm is great, just think on: when you have the ball, all eyes are on you and somebody else is already on their way to close you down!

Now, I don't want to dwell on a negative, but in the early stages it is likely that you will miss the ball. Everyone does it and it's all part of the game, but the important thing to remember is that once you've missed it, you're already late for your next job. It could be that you need to continue running because a team mate is about to pass it over your head, or maybe you need to double back into your original formation as everyone else behind has missed the ball as well. It is this instinct and sense of urgency about the next move that will give you an edge over a player who becomes distracted and consumed in his own disbelief when he misses the ball! Always focus on what your next job actually is, and take on board that it is rarely to dart back to a missed ball.

As hitting skill sets develop, it is beneficial to work on ball control and accuracy of passing. There will be a man on the pitch who has been given the job of marking you so the ability to release the ball quickly and accurately to a team mate becomes increasingly necessary.

I'm going to let you into a secret: as a beginner player, no-one really expects you to hit the ball, so you can enter the game with all of the pressure off!

Panicking or blind hitting vaguely in the direction you are hoping to score is risky and detrimental to your team objective – and we have already looked at the analogy of it being similar to a basketball player catching a ball and throwing it up the court just hoping that one that of his own team mates will get to it first!

In an effort to offer a bit of light relief, I'm going to let you into a secret: as a beginner player, no-one really expects you to hit the ball, so you can enter the game with all of the pressure off. In fact the reality is that in the early stages a new player is likely to be included in a game with other team members of a relatively similar ability who are quite keen for the others to miss because they want to have a crack at hitting the ball themselves!

When you first start to play it is vital that all players are aware of their own skill set, but equally you must know those of your team mates

It is hugely valuable to have a disciplined, committed team player who can be set the task of thoroughly marking their opposing player.

too. If a player with weak hitting skills is very confident in the riding department, then his job is to ride off the strongest opponent. If he is better at hitting, other team mates should be used to take away the dangerous opponents so that he can hit often and constructively.

I personally would much rather have a disciplined, competent rider on my team who is perhaps weak or inconsistent at hitting the ball. At least I can set them the task of thoroughly marking – and that's not just to neutralise the opposing player, but also it means I always know roughly where they are on the pitch because they will be tagging a more experienced player. So to follow are two areas of defensive play that will allow you to function as a valuable team player regardless of your actual hitting ability.

RIDING OFF

Riding off is permitted on both sides of the horse so long as the attacking player does not enter the 'airspace' that the stick will occupy during the course of a shot by the defending player. So timing and a well calculated execution are of uppermost importance.

Good ride offs are achieved when the intention is not just to spoil the opposition's shot but more so to remove him from the play altogether, rendering him useless for another play. And to do that you need to begin with a clear intention and a destination in your mind as to where you would like to ride him off to! A weak approach followed by a gentle 'bump' may not be sufficient for you to achieve anything at all other than mild amusement from your opponent and ultimately loss of the battle.

The ideal way to ride off is to collect and focus your energy, visually picturing a point three to five metres away on the opposite side of the player you are intending to ride off. Set yourself up with good rhythm and conviction, then at your chosen moment turn your shoulders and back to the player and drive your horse to the point you imagined. Ensure that you make contact at a compatible speed and an angle no greater than 45 degrees.

HOOKING

In the early stages of learning to play, it is always preferable to try to position yourself for a hooking option rather than a ride off. The main reasons being that you can often lose a ride off and several players will even have some clever sneaky tricks up their sleeves to manipulate a foul! The other reason is whilst a player is preoccupied on hitting the ball, you can focus all of your attention on riding alongside and making a hook. There are few defences against a well timed and executed homing of a mallet.

The trick to hooking is to be very clear visually in your mind of the right of way and direction of your opponent's horse, and also the airspace he is in and will be occupying when you reach him. Aim to ride to a point roughly two metres along side and parallel but just slightly ahead by a foot in length. It is this intention that will eliminate the sight often seen in low goal polo of enthusiastic players frantically swiping at a players stick but from behind!

"take one chukka four times a day...!"

Problem Solving

FAQ'S AND THE EXERCISES YOU NEED TO PUT THINGS RIGHT WITH YOUR PERFORMANCE AND HITTING

The good news about this section is that it's not a long one! If you have read this book from the start you will already have the answers. I can almost guarantee that any short-cutting and deviation from the pure essence of the physics will be at root of the problem.

As hitting skills progress, you will undoubtedly encounter some stumbling blocks. All of us are physically different and that is why it is so important to take those golden rules of hitting and adapt them to your own bodily make-up. It's already been explained that although it is hugely beneficial to watch good players, be careful if you try to adopt their style because it is specific to them. Find your own that works for you.

In my experience as you move along the learning curve, you will meet the same 'type' of problems that many other beginners face. So in an effort to help, I asked some of my new students to send in their problems. Here are the top thirteen things new students struggle with, followed by the shortened explanation of how to resolve them. Ideally you will need to study and apply the techniques outlined in previous relevant sections:

I MISS THE BALL A LOT...

Well, no short answer - go back to page one and read the book!

WHEN I STICK AND BALL, MY HORSE TURNS RIGHT WHEN I'M HITTING A BACKHAND DURING THE SWING...

This problem can occur for several reasons – the first is that as the body rotates to complete the follow-through, the rider is often taking the reins with him as well. As a result the horse will of course follow. The solution is to alter your intention on the approach. Imagine yourself traveling along a monorail: the track is straight and continuous and this is the direction you must follow – and no swing should ever interfere with the horse's movement. Learn to become more flexible and versatile in the saddle and give yourself a training aid such as the white line on the back of a pitch. Remove the ball from the scenario and put all of your focus on keeping the horse on, or parallel to the line, as you complete a series of backhand swings. Each one should be made up of a correct approach, a clean complete swing, and a continuation on the track. Once successful, re-introduce the ball, remembering to keep the focus on the direction you are travelling.

This problem can also occur when a rider has mistakenly taught the horse that he must indeed turn right during a swing. With enough constant repetition, a horse can easily pre-empt the next move, because remember: he feels you, but can't see you. In a player's enthusiasm to chase the backhand he has just hit or to get back to the one just missed, he will turn before the sequence of events is complete. The golden rule for any shot is to complete at least three whole strides on the approach to the ball and another three on the same track after the ball, regardless of whether it was hit or missed.

WHEN I HIT, THE STICK SPINS IN MY HAND...

At the moment of impact the arm, hand, and mallet should be travelling through a continuous plane that was initially accurately on course to hit the ball directly through its middle. If any one of these component parts is out of line then impact will be slightly off-centre, causing the mallet to twist.

The solution is to ensure that the riding position is able to accommodate a swinging mallet, and that the grip is correct to allow the mallet to become an extension of the arm. It is important to feel exactly how it should feel when everything is correct so you ultimately know what you are aspiring to.

Begin by adopting a half seat on the horse and lower the mallet head to the ground by pulling the left shoulder high and slightly backwards to simulate the position you should be in at the moment of impact. Open the fingers and allow the mallet handle to rest on the palm. Now spread the fingers wide and begin to close one at a time starting with little finger first.

The mallet head should remain 90 degrees to the horse and you can now place your chin on your chest. Hold the position for a while to log the feeling. Then using all of the mechanics of the body, draw the mallet backwards to a nine o'clock position. Manufacture the down swing back to the ball then draw it back up again. Repeat as many times as necessary to ensure that the muscle memory is correct on the final approach to the ball.

Remember: your intention is to ultimately swing **through the ball**, so finally complete the swing ensuring that the pendulum characteristics are clearly visible.

I CAN'T HIT THE BALL IN A STRAIGHT LINE…

ALL hitting directions are dictated by a plane. A plane is a pure thing that never deviates or falters from its course. The simple answer to this question is that the ball, once hit, will travel exactly in the direction of the plane that was initially established. The hand moving only a matter of inches away from a plane parallel to the horse will have an enormous influence on the degree left or right that it travels once hit. The inability to hit a ball in a straight line often arises if the technique being used is more of an 'aim and hit-at' rather than a complete 'swing through' from the right shoulder socket.

the finger shelf!

top tip.

excellent exercise to correct a multitude of hitting issues

Hold the stick with the middle, index finger and thumb only – the ring finger and little finger are placed under the stick handle for support almost acting like a shelf.

great way to fix lots of hitting problems!

A great exercise (that sorts many problems but especially this one) is to hold the stick with the middle, index finger, and thumb only – the ring finger and little finger are placed under the stick handle for support almost acting like a shelf. This position eliminates all opportunity to use strength during the shot and forces you to swing with the shoulder.

" I CAN'T GET MY BALLS TO LOFT...

Sending balls high into the air is fully dependent on the gradient and angle you brought the stick head down to the ball.

Perhaps many of you will be familiar with the effect of kicking a football – drawing the leg back and kicking the ball in its middle will send a ball forward and fairly low to the ground. However, if you were to aim and kick right underneath the ball with a chipping effect it will naturally climb higher. The same principle of 'getting underneath it' applies to a polo ball.

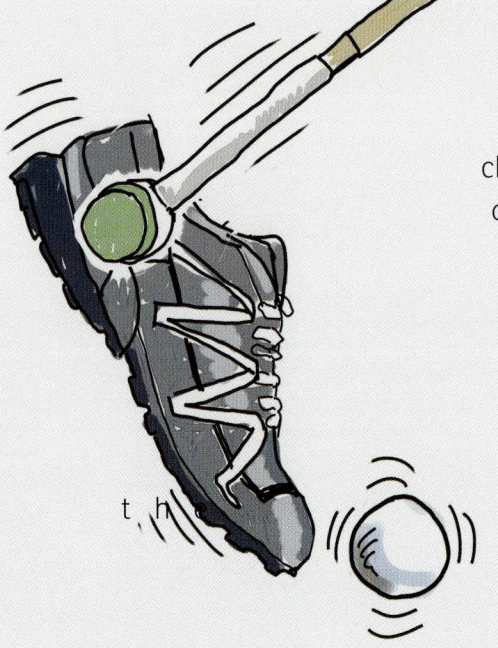

A technique that will dramatically improve performance actually begins with the ability to place the chin on the chest and stare directly and accurately down at the ball as if it was at the bottom of a tube. The tube technique requires a high degree of flexibility which, in turn, allows for the arm behind reaching higher above you enabling you to swing almost as if you wanted to drive the ball into ground.

I CAN'T GET DISTANCE ON MY BALLS...

All distance hitting is entirely down to the amount of energy / elasticity you are able to create within the body by twisting and rotating, and then being able to time the swing to perfection ensuring that all of that energy created transfers to the ball.

In basic principle, the further away from the ball you are able to get the stick head, the more momentum you will create to transfer. The essential way to create energy is to distort the body's natural frame work and stretch it to its furthest parts, and a very important part of this is to stack the left shoulder below the right hand. For example, the right arm reaching to an eleven or even midnight position would mean that the opposite left shoulder would need to be at a five or six o'clock position. You can experience the feeling you are meant to get just by standing still and applying the stacking method. What should now be clear is actually how much pelvic rotation is required because the pelvis and shoulders should effectively be fixed together in an invisible framework.

"oh allow me to show you..!"

Once the maximum or required amount of elasticity has been achieved, the feeling is almost as though you are hitting the ball into the ground rather than coming behind and hitting through it – similar to the previous example. All of the intensity created, coupled with all of the angles opening to straight, creates an explosion at the point of impact as the right side of the body powers through the ball. Very often you will see that whilst the integrity of the pendulum swing is still in place, the post-contact 'chest to the left' position will have been substituted for a square shoulder position as the player lofts the ball as if throwing his stick into the sky.

see pg 134!

> ## I CAN'T DO A STRAIGHT NEARSIDE...
>
> This one needs quite a lengthy explanation so probably best you review the whole section on the nearside! However in brief, the near side is only achievable when the right groin and right heel relationship is a good and sturdy one, allowing for a complete rotation of the pelvis. Once achieved, the right forearm and elbow can establish a plane parallel to the horse on the nearside.

The forearm will always dictate the direction the ball will ultimately travel.

I MISS WHEN I'M GOING QUICKER...

In a perfect world, you should train for the environment conditions you will be playing in. We have already identified the degree of versatility required in the saddle to correctly produce any of the basic shots. As the horse goes faster, it is highly likely that versatility in the saddle is greatly reduced as the player relies on his thighs and begins to grip the saddle. The immediate consequence is the inability to produce the 'hitting machine'. The second one is that the horse as it moves faster has more elevation, so it is higher off the ground during each stride, and an adjustment is required to lower the half seat.

Finally, as the horse gets quicker, there is a natural reaction to swing quicker. However, we know that **all** structured shots swing for a count of 'one and ...' for 1.5 seconds, regardless of whether they are established at eight, nine, ten, eleven or midnight, so discipline to feel for your pendulum characteristics and your checklist is essential on the approach to the ball at speed.

MY HORSE SLOWS WHEN I GO TO HIT...

With so many jobs to concentrate on in the early stages of hitting, it is understandable that some of them are forgotten. Unfortunately, one of the more common ones is to keep pressing the accelerator! Remember, if you can't get to the ball, you can't hit it. One of the first priorities of all hitting is consistency, and that also applies to the horse.

Consistency in his paces is paramount to aid you, the player, in timing the swing. On the approach to any ball, find a pace you are happy with and keep it going. Positive energetic riding does not necessarily involve speed, and it can be clearly identified in a walk, but try really hard not to fall into the trap of riding up to the ball then hit at, then ride off! Flow and ride through – remember, all hitting should be approached as if riding on a monorail with no stopping.

I CAN'T RESIST HITTING THE BALL HARD...

The initial answer to this one is to learn some discipline! However, the root of the problem can often go much deeper than that. People who consistently swing too fast have either absolutely no confidence in how the mechanics of the swing actually works (the result being that they have swapped all the technique for strength), or the preparation of the swing process was so late that in order to make contact the individual has no choice but to rush the shot. In each case, the discipline of coming back to basics to learn timing is essential, but in extreme cases, extreme solutions are required. Someone who swings very fast is presumably trying to get the ball to go very far. The reality is that whilst the ball may indeed travel, it will only travel as far as the hitter's strength allows.

The solution I have found that tames most of these speed hitters is plain old tissue paper. The technique is to scrunch tissue paper tightly into the size of polo balls and have them placed, on the 60 yard line. They won't actually travel any distance so there will be no point in hitting them hard. With that in mind all focus can now be on the quality of the swing.

problems at home?

On the approach in canter, drop the stick into a pendulum that reaches ten o'clock behind you five strides before the ball, counting 'one and...' for 1.5 seconds. Then take the same time to swing through the ball, ensuring that all characteristics of a true pendulum are visible and correct and finish at two o'clock. Continue with this exercise as many times as it takes until you are consistent with your timing.

Now comes the trick! Place several proper polo balls wrapped in tissue paper so they are unidentifiable amongst the others on the back line. On the approach, the rider will be unaware and totally focussed on producing yet another perfect swing as all the 'objects' look the same. The result will be miraculous. And at least now when the ball travels high and far without any energy, you will appreciate the results achieved when conforming to swinging correctly and relying on the pure physics!

THE BALL KEEPS GOING UNDER THE HORSE'S NECK WHEN I TAKE A NEARSIDE FOREHAND...

If you have read the section that contains the Smiley Grid, you will already have the answer to this problem. A ball when hit will travel in the direction of the plane that was initially established by the forearm and the elbow. Whilst many players may momentarily be able to establish a parallel forearm position to the horse, unless they maintain it as they swing, the bodily make up is guaranteed to pull the arm onto a new plane pointing to the right, similar to that of a tennis backhand.

The trick to maintaining the correct position for a straight nearside forehand is to simulate pulling the mallet down in a vertical motion almost as if it is in a tube. At the same time as it begins to unfold, keep forcing the elbow backwards. Sweep the mallet head along the floor and allow it to come to rest at the same height exactly opposite where it began.

MY HORSE MOVES AWAY WHEN I GO TO HIT...

This can happen for several reasons – fear of the stick, disobedience or simple 'self-preservation'! But it can also lie with a rider who is using the reins to balance on as he attempts to hit the ball. In all cases for both horse and rider, it is about revisiting the basics. A horse that moves away from a swing clearly has a few issues. Either he has been hit or nearly missed and likely both experiences have left him with fairly unpleasant memories. The trick, of course, is to fully restore his confidence in you and the polo mallet. In extreme cases, it is necessary to swing continuously without a ball and often only with a tapping motion. Once accepted, the size of the swing can be increased until he is calm and remains on a straight track for all shots. For some, this may only take a couple of minutes. For others, it could take hours, so be prepared to be patient and never become frustrated.

Remember, once you are on top of the horse, for the best part he can't actually see you – his senses intensify and he feels every single movement. A horse that moves away as you swing has remembered the feeling that when the human rotates the pelvis, the mallet is coming. If the problem lies with the rider, then absolute back-to-basic lessons are required, beginning on a lunge line. It is essential that a player can operate the mallet and balance independent of his hands.

MY HORSE SPEEDS UP WHEN I GO TO HIT...

There could be several explanations for this, but first decide whether this is a horse or a human problem. Does this horse speed up with every rider or just you? Do all the horses you play speed up on the approach to the ball? Firstly, it may be as simple as the half seat needs adjusting as it is possible that you are actually gripping the accelerator part of the horse with the lower legs by mistake as you roll into a half seat. The second likely cause is that as you approach the ball, the forward motion of the upper body is actually instructing the horse to accelerate as your reins move forward and give freedom of the horse's head and neck.

The other explanation lies with the horse. A horse that is played very often and rarely schooled will have a perception of polo in his mind. What is likely in this case is that when he feels the mallet swing and hears the noise of the ball being hit, he recalls all of the enthusiastic flapping of reins and kicking of legs to go chasing after it as fast as he can! While he may be able to distinguish between an energized playing environment and a quiet stick and ball session he is a horse and doesn't have the mental capability to rationalise. As far as he is concerned, the noise of you hitting the ball, or the feelings of body movement as you prepare to hit, is recognised as his signal to go faster. He is just doing what he always does and has never been told otherwise.

The solution: if the problem lies with a compromised half seat, practice trot to canter transitions in a half seat, making a huge effort to keep the lower legs off and away from the sides of the horse. This exercise will strengthen the thighs and allow the lower legs to become more independent, and to be used only when required, rather than as an essential part of staying on!

If the problem lies with the horse, then you must change his perception of his job. The easier solution as always is to strip it all down and come back to walk. Begin by hitting a ball, and as soon as he becomes excited or increases speed, turn him away and produce as many small circles as necessary until calm. He will soon learn that excitement means having to do a bit more work, and maintaining a consistent tempo will be rewarded with the luxury of continuing in a straight line.

Stretching

introducing the seven-minute stretch!!

Risking much controversy by suggesting you can indeed stretch successfully in the equivalent time that it takes to play a chukka, I decided to add this section anyway based on one specific fact:

Some stretching is better than no stretching at all! Equally controversial is why this section is at the back, but as I'm reliably informed by my own personal trainer it is as essential to warm down as it is to warm up.

In an ideal world, all players at any level will engage the help of a personal trainer to work on core, flexibility, and general fitness at times away from the pitch – it is a highly skilled and serious occupation so I will leave that job to the specialists. What I have done in this section is outline a routine devised by my own personal trainer who is also an accomplished player.

In recent years, as the sport has developed, so in turn have the ideologies. Rarely now will you find a serious high-goal team without their own pitch-side physio, personal trainer, or at the very least a stretching regime they adhere to religiously pre-match. Based on the sport you are about to play, much of the success of your performance will be based on your flexibility, so a couple of minutes taken out to warm up pre-chukka is invaluable and, more importantly, your horse will probably thank you for it.

So don't limit yourself to just seven minutes! Remember, the more you put in, the more you get out...

STRETCHING

Exercise One:
Polo Static Twist

Complete ten reps for thirty seconds

Exercise Two:
Shoulder Over Rotation

Complete ten reps for thirty seconds

Exercise Three:
Leg Kicking Forwards / Backwards

Complete ten each side, for thirty seconds each

STRETCHING
CONTINUED

Exercise Four:
Side Kicking

Complete ten each side, thirty seconds each

Exercise Five:
Lower Back Stretch

Rotate side-to-side for thirty seconds

Exercise Six:
Polo Stretch

Complete a thirty-second static stretch on each side

STRETCHING
CONTINUED

Exercise Eight:
Kneeling Polo Stretch

Complete thirty reps on each side.

Exercise Nine:
Bend-over Fingers

Complete a fifteen-second stretch on each side.

Exercise Ten:
Running on the Horse

The final part of this stretching routine actually takes place once you are mounted. Begin by removing the stirrups and stretch as far forward to the right as possible. Ensure that the right toe turns under the horse and the right groin touches the saddle. Aspire to lining up your shoulders above the horse's spine. Once you've found your maximum stretch, begin to draw the stick backwards, beginning with wrist backwards first, then elbow, then right shoulder. Simulate the feet being extremely heavy weights and kick them back, which in turn will drag the leg and thigh with them. This technique will produce an action almost as if running on the horse. It is a fast-track to warming up, as well as developing the core, groin, thighs, and overall stability.

you'll know you're doing it right because it really hurts!

And Finally...

Now that you've read the book you have everything you need to go out and play...

RUBBISH!

Polo is an extremely complex sport and requires an abundance of skill sets that need to come together to create a good player. Reading something does **not** mean that you can instantly go and do something perfectly. You need to understand how things work and practice good solid techniques until they become habitual. For some people, it may only take fifty repetitions of a specific exercise to ingrain essential muscle memory. For others, it may take five hundred. There is no magic number, so be clear on the exercise that you wish to master and practice, practice, practice and you **will** be rewarded with success.

You may recall that right at the beginning of the book we purposely looked at why children are naturals at learning to play polo. Their small stature allows them to harmonise with their horse; their lack of adult strength ensures they move and control the mallet with their bodily framework, and they swing the mallet like a sledge hammer. Additionally, many of them approach the ball in a relaxed frame of mind without any pressure or expectation of hitting it! It is exactly this child-like mindset and motion that you should be aspiring to – so that your overall theme is pure at its very core.

Whether you are completely new to the game or perhaps an amateur player encountering problems, you ideally need to 'feel how it feels' to be correct and **then** you will know what it is you are aspiring to. So like a child, your initial benchmark should be the feeling of **fluidity** through **both** the riding and hitting elements.

If you have followed the exercises in this book correctly, you should certainly be on the right track. I can guarantee, however, that any deviation from the pure physics will be at the root of all problems. So simply work out what and where the problem is, isolate it, and fix it by practicing the correct method and technique.

Remember: money can't buy skill. Only training can produce it! And above all, never forget:

It doesn't matter if you miss the ball...
it's polo, so you just need to **look fantastic!**

SO HAVE FUN, STAY SAFE, ENJOY YOUR TRAINING, AND SEE YOU ON THE PITCH!

and finally (again)
there are some people
I really need to thank...

Lee + Dazo

Jane

Philip Treacy model

The Stick Chicks

extra special thanks to Jane Palmer for her editing skills!

Valerie

More Stick Chicks

Rio off for chukkers

...for without their support and encouragement, this book would never have been possible...

thank you!

Acknowledgements

CONTRIBUTORS
Raja Abuljebain
Valerie Khasawneh
Mathieu Mondan
Dianne Breeze
Nico Petracchi
Mohammed Bin Drai
Henry Brett
Wael Soueid
Steve King
Alyazi Al Muhairi
Tim Wilkinson
Jake Hughes
Justo and Family
Maxi Malacalza
Guillermo Cuitino
Marco Focaccia
Gonzalo and Family
Nacho Gonzales
The Grooms

CREATIVE DIRECTOR
James Drinkwater

EDITORS
Sol Green
Marino Charientin
Adam Frith
Iain Grimes
Lee Slimming
Dazo Cashinella
Jane & Andy Palmer
Stuart Wrigley
Gary Shepherd

ILLUSTRATIONS
Dianne Breeze

PHOTOGRAPHY
Alice Gipps
Valerie Khasawneh
Annemieke Goos
Gonzalo Etcheverry
Riaz Siddiki

PLAYERS
Adolfo Cambiaso
Maximiliano Malacalza
Gonzalo Yanzon
Nicolas Petracchi
Guillermo Villanueva
Guillermo Cuitino
Facundo Castagnola
Nacho Gonzales
Salvador Ulloa
Alfredo Capella
Santiago Gomez Romero
Hugo Barabucci
Walter Garbuglia
Santiago Cernadas
Lucas Monteverde
Manolo Fernandez Llorente
Segundo Cavanagh
Rodolfo Ducos
Juan Jose Brane
Felipe Martinez Ferrario
Fecundo Fernandez Llorente
Diego T. Cavanagh
Segundo Amadori
Mohammed Bin Drai
Raja Abuljebain